English for
Nursing

Vocational English
Course Book

D0074334

Maria Spada Symonds and Ros Wright

Series editor David Bonamy

Contents

Patient admissions

- talk about hospital jobs and personn
- talk about hospital departments and
  facilities
- handle admissions
- check in a patient

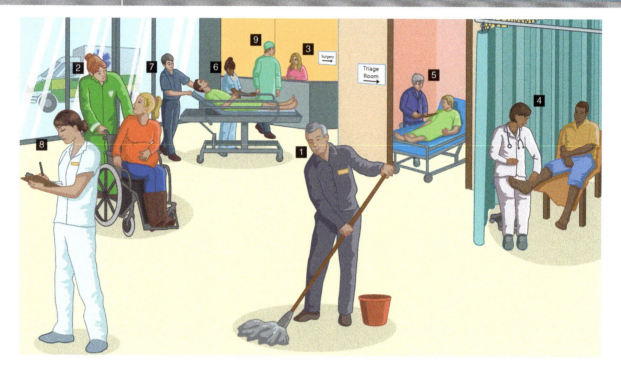

Hospital jobs and personnel

Vocabulary

1 Look at the picture and match the job titles a–i with the hospital personnel 1–9.

a) ☐ charge nurse / sister   d) ☐ paramedic   g) ☐ surgeon

b) ☐ cleaner   e) ☐ porter   h) ☐ triage nurse

c) ☐ consultant   f) ☐ receptionist   i) ☐ scrub nurse

2 Read and choose the best description 1–9 for each job in 1.

1 I'*m responsible for* keeping the patient rooms clean.

2 I *give* emergency *treatment* to accident victims and then transport them to hospital by ambulance.

3 I *deal with* patient details and check their hospital records.

4 I am a senior doctor and I *specialise in* a certain area of medicine.

5 I'*m responsible for* making sure the most urgent cases are treated by the doctor as quickly as possible.

6 I *look after* patients during surgery and after their operations.

7 I *assist* the medical staff by transporting patients from one department to another.

8 I *am responsible for* running a ward. I *deal with* budgets and with employing staff.

9 I *carry out* operations on patients. I usually *specialise in* a particular type of surgery.

Language

Reading **3** Read the interview with a practice nurse and underline the correct verb forms.

Reena Chaudry: *practice nurse*

AGE: 33 years old   HOME: Hyderabad, India

'I ¹*work / 'm working* as a practice nurse in a big doctor's surgery. This is my first job since graduation. I ²*like / 'm liking* the fact that every day is different. Practice nurses ³*carry out / are carrying out* a lot of routine procedures; they ⁴*change / are changing* dressings and ⁵*treat / are treating* wounds, etc. I ⁶*am / am being* also responsible for giving health checks and advising patients; I ⁷*give / 'm giving* them advice on healthy eating, for example and on health conditions such as asthma or diabetes. At the moment, with a colleague, we ⁸*run / are running* a clinic for patients with diabetes. It's very interesting. and I ⁹*learn / 'm learning* a lot about how to deal with this condition. Like most nurses, I ¹⁰*don't have / 'm not having* a lot of free time, but I ¹¹*like going / 'm liking going* to the cinema when I can. I also ¹²*play / 'm playing* the sitar in a classical music group.'

Listening **4**   02   You're going to hear an interview with Carlos da Silva. Listen and answer this question.

Carlos da Silva: *agency nurse*

AGE: 35 years old   HOME: Auckland, New Zealand

What area of nursing does he specialise in?
a) renal care
b) paediatrics
c) emergency medicine

5 Listen again. Copy and complete the sentences about Carlos.

1 He specialises in ...
2 At the moment, he's working in ...
3 He's looking after ...
4 Every day, he ...
5 This week, he's ...
6 In his job, he likes / doesn't like ...
7 In the future, he hopes to ...
8 In his free time ...

Speaking **6** Work in pairs. Take turns to choose one of the sentences in 5 and ask your partner questions. Then introduce your partner to the class.

Hospital departments and facilities

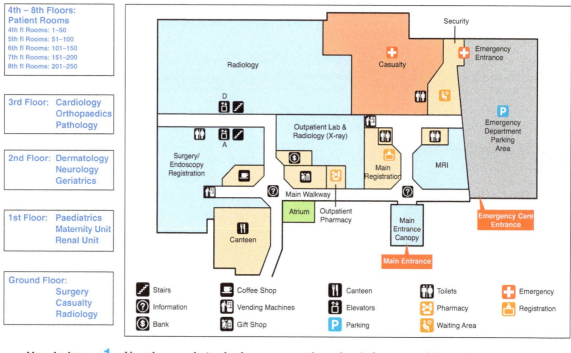

4th – 8th Floors:
Patient Rooms
4th fl Rooms: 1–50
5th fl Rooms: 51–100
6th fl Rooms: 101–150
7th fl Rooms: 151–200
8th fl Rooms: 201–250

3rd Floor: Cardiology
Orthopaedics
Pathology

2nd Floor: Dermatology
Neurology
Geriatrics

1st Floor: Paediatrics
Maternity Unit
Renal Unit

Ground Floor:
Surgery
Casualty
Radiology

Key:
Stairs · Information · Bank · Coffee Shop · Vending Machines · Gift Shop · Canteen · Elevators · Parking · Toilets · Pharmacy · Waiting Area · Emergency · Registration

Vocabulary 1 Use the words in the box to complete the definitions of these hospital departments.

> babies   children   elderly   emergency cases   exercises   heart   kidney
> nervous system   operations   skin disorders   test results   X-rays

1 **Casualty** is the place where they treat _____ .
2 **Surgery** is where surgeons carry out _____ .
3 Medical staff in the **Renal** Unit specialise in _____ diseases.
4 The **Dermatology** Department is where they deal with _____ .
5 Specialists in **Geriatrics** treat problems related to the _____ .
6 **Pathology** is where they analyse patient _____ .
7 Midwives deliver _____ in the **Maternity** Unit.
8 **Paediatrics** is where they treat _____ .
9 Patients with _____ disease visit **Cardiology.**
10 The **Radiology** Department is where they take _____ .
11 Disorders of the _____ are treated in the **Neurology** Department.
12 In the **Physiotherapy** Department, patients learn special _____ to help them recover.

Pronunciation 2 🔊 **03** Put the words in bold from 1 into the correct box according to their stress pattern. Then listen and check your answers. Listen again and repeat.

●·	●··	·●··	··●·	··●··	···●··
	Surgery			*Dermatology*	

Speaking 3 Work in pairs. Take turns to ask and answer questions about the location of other places in the hospital. Use questions like these.

Excuse me; I'm looking for the …

Sorry, where is / are the …?

Do you know where the … is / are?

Vocabulary

4 A Senior Staff Nurse is explaining the layout of the hospital. Choose the correct prepositions in italics to complete the explanations 1–6.

1 The Dermatology Department is *between / at* the Neurology Department *at / and / in* Geriatrics.
2 Room 246 is *at / in / on* the eighth floor, just on *in front of / the left of* the lift.
3 You can find the Renal Unit *at / in / on* the first floor, *opposite / at* Paediatrics.
4 Your wife is *at / in / on* the Maternity Unit *at / in / on* the end of the corridor.
5 The Geriatrics Department is *next to / between* the Dermatology Department *at / in / on* the second floor.
6 I think that Mrs Nguyan is sitting over there, *between / in front of* the vending machine.

5 Match the symbols a–i with the facilities 1–9.

1 canteen	4 pharmacy	7 cashpoint
2 registration desk	5 waiting area	8 toilets
3 vending machine	6 coffee shop	9 gift shop

Listening

6 🔊 04 You are going to hear people giving directions to different hospital facilities. Listen and complete the instructions.

1
Visitor: Excuse me; I'm looking for the canteen. Can you help me?
Nurse: Yes of course. Go _____ _____ and it's in _____ _____ you, _____ the _____ of the corridor.

2
Visitor: Excuse me, do you know where the Maternity Unit is?
Nurse: It's on the _____ floor. Turn _____ here, go straight on, and when you get to the information desk, _____ right. At the end _____ the corridor, _____ _____ again and take elevator A. The Maternity Unit is the first door on the left.

3
Visitor: Hello. Do you know if there's a shop in the building? We want to buy some magazines.
Nurse: Sure. Just _____ _____ here and _____ down the corridor, there's a gift shop _____ _____ the pharmacy. You can buy magazines there, I think.

7 🔊 05 Look at the hospital plan on page 6. Listen to the directions from this nurse and follow the plan with your finger. Then circle the correct answer.

1 The visitor is looking for the *coffee shop / main entrance / canteen*.
2 The visitor is on the *1st / 3rd / 4th* floor.

8 Look at audio script 5 on page 70 and check your answers.

Admissions

Reading **1** Read the extract from a patient information leaflet from the Central Hospital in Phoenix, Arizona in the USA. What is the average waiting time ...

1 for a patient in ER in Central Hospital?
2 for a patient in ER in the State of Arizona?

Central Hospital

What to Expect

Highly skilled and experienced emergency medical staff are on hand 24 hours a day, seven days a week to provide essential emergency care at the Central Hospital Emergency Room (ER).

The Triage Process

At the ER, we treat patients whose lives are in danger first. A special nurse 'sorts' the other patients and puts them in order according to how bad their symptoms are. This is called triage.

When you arrive, this is usually what happens:

You check in at the [1]_____ .

You give your name, address and [2]_____ , etc.

You wait in a [3]_____ .

A [4]_____ carries out some basic tests (pulse, heart rate, etc.)

He / She asks you some questions and makes an initial [5]_____ of your condition.

He / She decides the [6]_____ of care of all the patients in his / her charge.

The doctor visits you in the [7]_____ as soon as he / she is available.

The Order of Care

We treat patients in order of priority:

Emergency (life-threatening) conditions, e.g. [8]_____ .

Urgent problems, e.g. [9]_____ .

Non-urgent problems, e.g. [10]_____ .

Waiting Times in ER

If your condition is not serious, you may have to wait before seeing a doctor in ER. However, our policy is to give quality care as soon as possible to all our patients. That is why at Central Hospital patients typically spend two hours less waiting in ER than the state average of 4.5 hours.

---

2 Read the leaflet again. Complete the gaps 1–7 in the 'When you arrive' section with the words in the box.

> assessment   cubicle (x2)   date of birth   priority   reception desk   triage nurse

3 Look at these medical problems a–c. Which are the most serious? Match them to gaps 8–10 in the 'Order of care' section. Compare your answers with a partner.

a) problems with breathing, a broken bone
b) earache, sore throat
c) heart attack, stopped breathing.

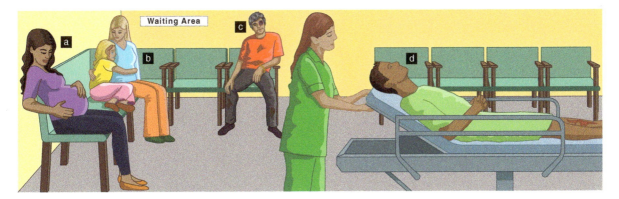

Listening **4** 🔊 **06** Listen to a triage nurse talking to four new patients. Decide which patient a–d above is speaking.

Patient 1 _____   Patient 3 _____
Patient 2 _____   Patient 4 _____

5 Listen again and complete the sentences with the words in the box.

baby	bleeding	eye	hurts	leg	worried

1 He has problems with his left _____ .
2 Her head is _____ a lot.
3 My head _____ .
4 I'm _____ about the _____ .
5 My _____ hurts.

6 Work in pairs. Put the patients in order of priority to see the doctor. Compare your ideas with another pair.

7 Match the sentence halves to make six requests.

1 Could you take a seat in	a) lie back and try to relax?
2 Could you fill in	b) your head?
3 Could you	c) a few questions, please?
4 Could you tell me	d) this form, please?
5 Could you show me	e) the waiting room, please?
6 Could I just ask you	f) what happened?

8 Listen again to the dialogue and choose one of the requests from 7 for each patient a–d. Compare your ideas with a partner.

Pronunciation **9** 🔊 **07** Can you pronounce the letters of the alphabet in English? Complete the groups with letters that have the same sound. Listen and check your answers.

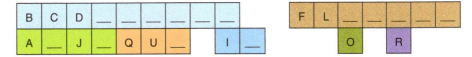

10 Write down the names of four people you know. Work in pairs. Take turns to spell the names to each other.

Checking in a patient

Vocabulary

Birmingham General Hospital

Patient Details

Title: .... First name(s): .... Surname: ....

Gender: ☐ M ☐ F   Marital status: ....

DOB: .... Country of origin: ....

Occupation: ....

Address: *53 Coalport Ave, Tipton, Birmingham B32 9AH* ....

Tel: (home) .... (work) *020 832 9400* .... (mobile) *0779 003 5491*

GP: *Dr Alice White* .... Tel: *020 612 1398* ....

Next of kin: .... Relationship to patient: *husband* ....

Tel: (home) *020 831 9476* .... (mobile) ....

Smoking intake: *n/a* .... Allergies: ....

Reason for admission: *7 months pregnant, possible ...* ....

1 Find the words in the admissions form with these meanings.

1 family name _____
2 job _____
3 Mr / Mrs / Ms / Dr _____
4 family doctor _____
5 the name the patient wants the medical staff to use _____
6 closest relative _____
7 country where patient was born _____
8 male or female _____
9 married / single / divorced / widowed _____
10 why the patient is visiting hospital _____
11 date of birth _____
12 the amount of something you drink / eat, etc. regularly _____
13 a bad reaction to, for example, food or medicine _____

Listening **2** 🔘 **08** You are going to hear the nurse interview a patient from 4 on page 9. Listen. Which patient is she talking to? Listen again and fill in the admissions form for the patient.

3 Listen again and complete the nurse's questions.

1 Can you give me your full _____ please?
2 Can you _____ that, please?
3 What would you like us to _____ you?
4 What is your _____ of _____ ?
5 What is your _____ ?
6 Do you have any _____ ?

4 Write questions for these answers. Look at audio script 8 on page 70 to check your answers.

1 Where _____ ?
 I'm originally from Catagne, in Sicily.
2 What's _____ ?
 I'm married.
3 Who _____ ?
 That's Daniel, my husband.

Vocabulary **5** The doctor decides that Rosanna is going to stay in hospital for observation. Look at her room. Label the picture with the words in the box.

| bed | buzzer | chair | drawer |
| light | locker | table | TV |

Listening **6** 🔊 09 Listen and write the names of the objects from 5 that you hear.

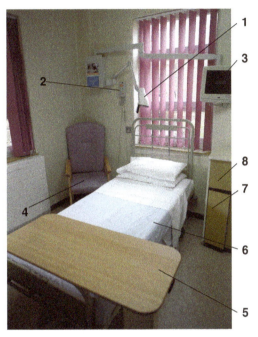

7 Listen again. Then look at the photo and complete the information about the facilities in the room and hospital.

1 The buzzer is next to the _____ above the _____ .
2 The _____ is next to the window, on the right.
3 The _____ is above the locker.
4 The gift shop is between the _____ and the _____ .
5 The gift shop is on the _____ floor.
6 The public phone is down the _____ , on the left after the _____ .

Speaking **8** Work in pairs. Take turns playing the role of a patient and of the nurse who admits the patient to hospital. Invent an identity for your patient, including the details below. Copy a blank patient admissions form like the one on page 10. Interview your patient and complete their details in the form. Then show the patient to their bed and explain the facilities in the room.

- full name and address
- family and next of kin
- date and place of birth
- occupation
- marital status
- smoking intake
- allergies
- reason for admission

2 Pain

- locate and describe pain
- assess pain
- communicate successfully
- talk about pain relief

Locating and describing pain

Vocabulary

1 Label the pain map using the words in the box

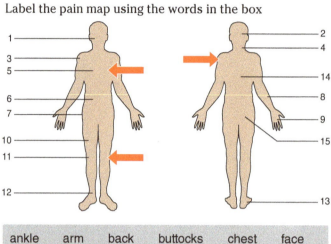

ankle	arm	back	buttocks	chest	face
foot	hand	head	hip	knee	leg	neck
shoulder	stomach

Verb	Noun	Adjective
My head hurts.		
My head aches.	I've got a headache.	
	I've got a pain in my head.	It's painful.
		His head is sore.

2 Rewrite sentences 1–6 so they have the same meaning, but use different words from the table in 1.

1 I've got a terribly sore throat and I think I've got a temperature.
2 I hurt my ankle this morning, running up the stairs. It's still very painful.
3 Have you got a headache? You don't look very well.
4 Ah, poor thing. Her gums really hurt. Her teeth are coming through.
5 He's got stomach ache. I don't think that chicken was properly cooked.
6 I've got a pain in my lower back and it's really aching. It's from carrying my computer.

3 Write at least one sentence for each red arrow in 1 to answer the question: How do you feel?

4 🔊 10 Where do the patients feel pain? Put a cross (✗) on the pain map for each patient.

1 James _____ 2 Godfrey _____ 3 Alma _____

5 Complete these expressions to give the exact location of the pain and the question that the nurse asks to get this information.

1 James: It's _____ the chest and the _____ .
2 Godfrey: It's on the _____ side, just _____ the eye.
3 Alma: It's at the _____ of the _____ and then shoots _____ the leg.
4 Nurse: _____ do you _____ the pain?

6 Put these words in order to make sentences that patients can use to describe how their pain changes.

1 pain / The / much / is / now / better   ↗ _____
2 better / I / today / feel   ↗ _____
3 than / worse / yesterday / It's   ↘ _____
4 my leg / worse / in / is / The / much / pain ↘ _____

Language

Comparatives and superlatives

We use comparative adjectives to compare two people or things.
We use superlative adjectives to compare a person or thing with a number of other people or things.

	Adjective	Comparative (+ than)	Superlative
one syllable and most two-syllable adjectives	strong	stronger	the strongest
longer adjectives	severe, painful	more severe, more painful	the most severe, the most painful
irregular adjectives	good, bad	better, worse	the best, the worst

*My backache is **more painful** today **than** yesterday.*   *I feel **better** now **than** I did this morning.*

7 Use the adjectives in the table above to complete the patient's descriptions of their pain.

1 It always begins with a pain on the left side of my head, which gets
  stronger and ¹_____ and then I start to feel nauseous. I have to take
  painkillers and lie down in a darkened room. I start to feel ²_____ after
  about an hour or so and by the next day I'm generally ³_____ . For me
  the ⁴_____ case ever lasted for seventy-two hours. On a scale of nought
  to ten, it's a ten. It's ⁵_____ pain I know.
2 I get this pain all around my forehead and behind my cheekbones. The
  problem is ¹_____ when I have a cold, so it's worse in the winter than
  the summer, but the ²_____ was last year when I was pregnant. I find
  the ³_____ treatment is a nasal spray, but I also feel ⁴_____ if I use a
  warm face pack.

8 Choose the correct medical problem for each patient description in 7.

1 a) food allergies b) migraine c) sinusitis d) backache
2 a) food allergies b) migraine c) sinusitis d) backache

Pain assessment

1   Mr Turner _____
2   Abdul _____
3   Shazia _____
4   Mrs Chen _____
5   Karin _____

Listening **1** [🔊 11] Listen to five patients talking about their pain. Write down the area where each patient feels the pain.

2 Listen again. Complete the sentences the patient uses to describe the pain with the words in the box.

| burning | dull | shooting | stabbing | tingling | throbbing |

1   I still have a headache. It's like a drum, a real _____ pain.
2   There's a _____ ache in my lower back. It's quite a mild pain, but sometimes I can feel a _____ pain, like an electric shock.
3   I get this _____ feeling two or three hours after food and sometimes it's very sore.
4   It's a kind of _____ feeling, like pins and needles. I get it in my feet as well, but it's better than last week
5   Yes, it's a _____ pain, like a knife. It's a severe pain. It really hurts a lot.

Vocabulary **3** Match the adjective phrases 1–8 with the descriptions a–h.

Adjective	Description
1 a burning sensation	a) It feels like someone is beating a drum.
2 a dull ache	b) It feels like someone is hurting me with a knife or something sharp.
3 a shooting pain	c) It feels like I want to scratch.
4 a stabbing pain	d) It feels like a bee is stinging me.
5 a tingling feeling	e) It feels very hot.
6 a throbbing pain	f) It feels like someone is pushing lots of small needles in your skin.
7 a stinging sensation	g) It's a sudden pain that moves quickly from one place to another.
8 not a pain, but itchy	h) It's a mild pain that is continuous.

4 Match the expressions in the box with the faces and the numbers on the chart.

mild pain	moderate pain	no pain	severe pain	unbearable pain

very severe pain

0 — 0–10 ← 1 _____

2 ← 2 _____

3 ← 3 _____

4 ← 4 _____

5 _____

6 _____

Speaking

5 Add a Wh- question word to 1–8 to form pain assessment questions.

1 _____ does it hurt?

2 _____ long does the pain last?

3 _____ did it start?

4 _____ do you feel?

5 _____ is the pain?

6 _____ does the pain move to?

7 _____ does the pain feel like?

8 _____ do you have pain?

6 Work in pairs. Student A, look at the information below. Student B, turn to page 68. Student A, you are the patient Tony / Antonia Bates. Student B will interview you about your pain. When you have finished, swap roles. Interview Student B and complete the pain map and pain scale below.

Patient case ....

You are Tony / Antonia Bates and you are suffering from stabbing pains in the middle of your chest that started at 10am today. The pain was unbearable (9 / 10 on the pain scale). It moves across the chest to the right arm. It feels as though you are being stabbed with a knife. You feel better now (7 / 10) than at 10am.

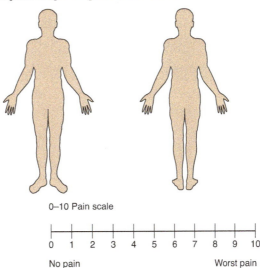

0–10 Pain scale

0 1 2 3 4 5 6 7 8 9 10

No pain   Worst pain

7 Work in different pairs. What kind of pain do you think the conditions below might cause? Discuss the location and the severity of the pain. Compare your ideas with another pair.

1 labour
2 appendicitis
3 severe migraine

4 broken shoulder
5 kidney stones
6 tonsillitis

Successful communication

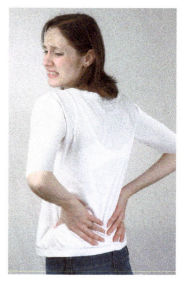

Listening **1** 🔊 **12** Practice Nurse David Taylor is assessing Dina Guyader, age 28. Listen to Part 1 of the pain assessment and answer the questions.

    1 Where is the pain?
    2 What sort of pain is it? Describe it.

2 🔊 **13** Listen to Part 2 of the assessment and put a cross and a letter on the pain scale to indicate:

    1 how Dina feels now (N).
    2 how Dina feels in the morning (M).

```
|---|---|---|---|---|---|---|---|---|---|
 0   1   2   3   4   5   6   7   8   9  10
No pain                            Worst pain
```

3 Listen again and choose the correct answers.

    1 How many children does Dina have?
       a) one   b) two   c) three
    2 What is Dina's employment situation?
       a) She works full time.   b) She works part time.   c) She is unemployed.
    3 What does Nurse Taylor learn about Dina's husband?
       a) He is unemployed.   b) He travels abroad a lot.
       c) He lives abroad.

Writing **4** Nurses often use an initial pain assessment tool to help them assess their patients' pain. Look at the extract below and complete 1–3.

    1 Rewrite question 5 with the verb *to make better*.
    2 Rewrite question 6 with the verb *to make worse*.
    3 Match the symptoms in the box with the correct sections in question 7.

> anger can't climb stairs easily can't do sports can't eat
> can't stand even for short periods crying insomnia ~~nausea~~ suicidal feelings

---

INITIAL PAIN ASSESSMENT TOOL   **Patient name:** *Dina Guyader*

5 What relieves the pain?   _____

6 What increases the pain?   _____

7 Effects of pain
    Accompanying symptoms   e.g. *nausea* _____
    Sleep   e.g. _____
    Appetite   e.g. _____
    Physical activity   e.g. _____
    Emotions   e.g. _____

Listening **5** 🔊 **14** Listen to Part 3 of Dina's assessment and complete the initial pain assessment tool with her details. Work in pairs and compare your ideas.

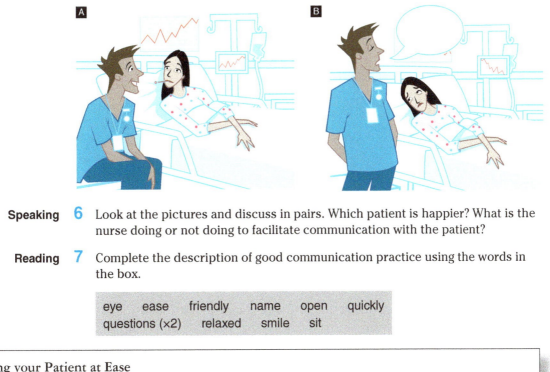

A

B

Speaking 6 Look at the pictures and discuss in pairs. Which patient is happier? What is the nurse doing or not doing to facilitate communication with the patient?

Reading 7 Complete the description of good communication practice using the words in the box.

eye	ease	friendly	name	open	quickly
questions (×2)		relaxed	smile	sit	

Putting your Patient at Ease

Good communication with your patient is essential. Imagine the patient is a close family member or friend and treat him or her as you wish to be treated yourself. Always try to put your patient at [1]_____ and make them feel [2]_____ . If possible, [3]_____ at the same level as the patient. The expression on your face is important, so [4]_____ and maintain [5]_____ contact with your patient. When you talk, don't rush the patient or speak too [6]_____ and always use a [7]_____ , open tone of voice. Take an interest in your patient, use their [8]_____ and ask them general [9]_____ about their life. It is also important to use an [10]_____ posture, i.e. don't fold your arms, as this can look aggressive. Finally, check it is OK to ask [11]_____ and tell them roughly how long the interview will last.

Pronunciation 8 🔊 15 Listen and tick (✓) if these nurses sound friendly or unfriendly when greeting their patients.

	Friendly	Unfriendly		Friendly	Unfriendly
Nurse 1	✓		Nurse 3		
Nurse 2			Nurse 4		

9 🔊 16 Complete the 'rule' then listen and repeat the pattern you hear.
A friendly welcome usually uses:

〜〜〜〜〜➔ ... an intonation pattern that rises and falls.
————➔ ... a flat intonation.

Speaking 10 Read audio scripts 12, 13 and 14 on pages 71–72. Find and underline these examples of how the nurse tries to put Dina at ease. Write what he says in each case.

1 He uses the patient's name.
2 He asks about the baby's health.
3 He checks the baby is OK.
4 He gives Dina the time she needs.
5 He shows empathy / understanding.
6 He checks it is OK to ask questions.

Pain relief

1 Work with a partner. How many types of pain relief can you think of for a patient with lower back pain? Make a list. Which do you think are the most effective and the least effective? Why?

2 Read and complete this article from a health website with the words in the box.

anti-inflammatory	comfortable position	heat patches
hot-water bottle	ice pack	muscles	painkillers	pillow
shower	swimming

Lower back pain

Follow this treatment and most lower back pain will improve:

1 Rest in a ^{1}_____ for the first 1–2 days. You can lie on your side with a ^{2}_____ between your knees, or on your back on the floor with it under your knees. Take a ^{3}_____ (10–20 minutes) every 2–3 hours, then rest in a comfortable position.

2 Take ^{4}_____ such as paracetamol, or an ^{5}_____ such as ibuprofen. These medicines usually work best if you take them regularly and not when the pain is serious.

3 Use a ^{6}_____ for 15–20 minutes, every 2–3 hours. You could also buy ^{7}_____ that last for a maximum of eight hours. Or you could try an ^{8}_____ for 10–15 minutes every 2–3 hours.

4 Return to normal activities as soon as possible. It is important that you don't stay in bed for more than 1–2 days, as your ^{9}_____ become weak and this worsens the problem.

5 The best exercise for the lower back is walking, beginning with 5–10 minutes a day. Another good form of exercise for lower back pain is ^{10}_____ in shallow water.

3 Write *Do* or *Don't* to complete the advice for the patient.

Example: *1 Don't stay in the same position too long.*

1 _____ stay in the same position too long.
2 _____ take pain medication before the pain becomes really bad.
3 _____ use heat or ice to help reduce the pain.
4 _____ stay in bed for more than two days.
5 _____ go for short walks.

4 Work in pairs. Take turns asking and responding to these questions.

1 Heat patches are expensive. What can I use instead?
2 I don't like walking. Can you suggest another exercise for me?
3 I still have back pain after two weeks. What can I do?

5 Work in small and groups and discuss this question.

Do you find the article in 2 helpful for patients? Why / why not?

a Hypnotherapy

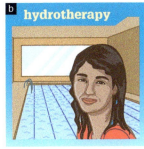
b hydrotherapy

aromatherapy

d herbal therapy

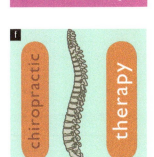
e music therapy

f chiropractic therapy

Vocabulary 6 Some patients choose to use complementary and alternative medicine (CAM) to treat their pain. Match the different examples of CAM a–f with the descriptions 1–6.

1 The therapist uses sound to help relax the muscles and improve the patient's mental well-being. _____

2 This therapy uses natural oils to help control pain, sometimes through massage. _____

3 The therapist gives advice on underwater exercise to help treat pain and injury. _____

4 This therapy uses herbs and plants to help treat medical problems including muscle ache and pain. _____

5 The therapist manipulates the bones in the spine to help treat pain. _____

6 The therapist talks to the patient when he or she is 'asleep' to influence their feelings about pain. _____

Listening 7 🔊 17 You are going to hear Angie and Carlos talking about their experiences using CAM. As you listen, tick (✓) the examples of CAM that you hear.

1 ☐ aromatherapy   4 ☐ hydrotherapy

2 ☐ chiropractic therapy   5 ☐ hypnotherapy

3 ☐ herbal therapy   6 ☐ music therapy

8 Listen again. Are these sentences *true* (T) or *false* (F)? Correct the false statements.

1 Angie only takes medication when the pain is really strong. (T / F)

2 Carlos knows that ginger can be used for pain relief. (T / F)

3 Angie agrees that swimming is a good way to relieve pain. (T / F)

4 Angie wants to try chiropractic therapy. (T / F)

5 Carlos believes CAM is only effective for chronic pain. (T / F)

Vocabulary 9 Complete these definitions. Give two more examples for each.

1 Chronic pain _____ . It can be caused by lower back pain, _____ and _____ .

2 Acute pain _____ . Examples include: dental work, _____ and _____ .

Speaking 10 In small groups, discuss these questions.

1 How are CAM viewed in your country / place of work?

2 What is your experience of CAM – either as a patient or as a nurse?

Vital signs

- describe statistics and vital signs
- describe readings
- take vital signs
- talk about circulation and the heart

Statistics and vital signs

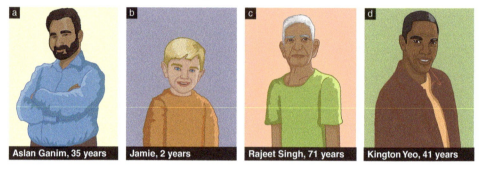

Aslan Ganim, 35 years | Jamie, 2 years | Rajeet Singh, 71 years | Kington Yeo, 41 years

Listening

1 🔊 **18** Listen to a practice nurse weighing and measuring her patients. Circle the correct number.

1 1.16 m / 1.60 m
2 72 kg / 62 kg
3 1.34 m / 1.24 m
4 89.95 kg / 89.5 kg
5 22.25 kg / 22.5 kg
6 1.14 m / 1.40 m

2 🔊 **19** Nurse McMaster is weighing and measuring patients in Admissions. Listen and match the dialogues 1–4 with the patients a–d.

3 Listen again and plot the height and weight of patients 1–3 on the chart. Label each patient as obese, overweight, underweight or normal weight.

4 Complete the nurse's questions. If necessary, listen again to check.

1 _____ _____ empty your bladder _____ ?

2 How tall _____ _____ ?

3 What's your _____ in metres?

4 Can you just _____ on the _____ for me, please?

5 How _____ do you _____ normally?

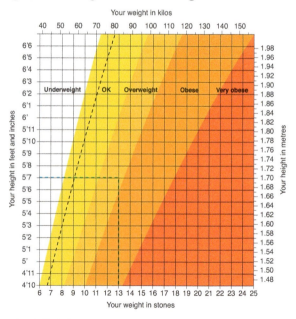

5 Work in pairs. Take it in turns to weigh and measure each other. Swap partners and weigh and measure another student in the class.

1 cm = 0.393 inches
1 m = 3.28 feet
1 kg = 2.20 pounds or 0.157 stone

Vocabulary   **6**   Match these vital signs 1–4 with the correct definitions a–d.

1   blood pressure   a) how many times a person breathes per minute
2   pulse   b) how hot the body is
3   rate of respiration   c) how many times the heart beats per minute
4   temperature   d) the force with which blood travels round the body

7   Label the pictures of medical equipment with the words in the box. What is each piece of equipment used to measure? Write sentences.

A stethoscope is used to measure …

> digital blood pressure monitor   pulseoximeter
> sphygmomanometer   stethoscope   thermometer

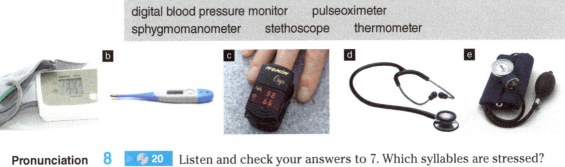

Pronunciation   **8**   🔊 **20**   Listen and check your answers to 7. Which syllables are stressed? Underline the stressed syllables in each word.

1   digital blood pressure monitor   4   stethoscope
2   thermometer   5   sphygmomanometer
3   pulse oximeter

9   Listen again and repeat.

Speaking   **10**   Work in pairs. Match the abbreviations on the chart with the words in the box. Which instruments from 7 are used to take these measurements? Explain the abbreviations to your partner.

Example: *RR stands for / means …*   *We use a … to measure / record this.*

> blood pressure   kilograms   oxygen   oxygen saturation   percentage
> pulse   respiration rate   temperature   weight

Patient name: *Alberto Riviera*

Date/ Time	BP	P	RR	T	Wt	O₂ Sats	Signature
14.10.11	130 / 80	75	15	37	71 kg	96%	R. Perez

Vocabulary   **11**   Complete the summary with the words in the box. Compare your answers with a partner.

> high   low   monitor   observation chart   record   sign   take   vital signs

Nurses usually ¹_____ the patient's ²_____ several times a day. We ³_____ the information on the ⁴_____ and ⁵_____ it. Medical staff then use this information to ⁶_____ the patient. If there are any changes, a ⁷_____ temperature (fever), for example, or a ⁸_____ blood pressure count, we have to inform the Senior Staff Nurse immediately.

Describing readings

Vocabulary **1** Match the statistics with the vital signs. Put a tick (✓) in the correct column.

	RR	BP	P	T
130 / 85				
36.8				
79				
20				

2 Complete the descriptions of the vital signs with the words in the box.

at	one	over	per (×2)	point

1 BP is _____ thirty _____ eighty-five.
2 Resps are _____ twenty breaths _____ minute.
3 Temperature is thirty-six _____ eight.
4 Pulse is seventy-nine beats _____ minute.

Listening **3** 🔊 **21** Listen and complete the readings you hear.

1

Patient name: *Mr Eric Jamieson*				Date of birth: *19.02.53*		
BP	**P**	**RR**	**T**	**Wt**	**O₂ Sats**	**Signature**
120 / 80				*93 kg*	*94%*	*Y. Leaming*

2

Patient name: *Mr Daniel Samson*				Date of birth: *10.08.71*		
BP	**P**	**RR**	**T**	**Wt**	**O₂ Sats**	**Signature**
				75 kg	*95%*	*J. Arrighi*

4 🔊 **22** Listen to a reading with some mistakes in it. Correct the mistakes you hear.

Patient name: *Anja Wellington*				Date of birth: *21.11.2002*		
BP	**P**	**RR**	**T**	**Wt**	**O₂ Sats**	**Signature**
98 / 65	*100*	*23*	*37.2*	*32 kg*	*98%*	*B. Guzman*

Speaking **5** Put the words in the box in the correct column in the table. Discuss the ways in which each of these factors can affect a patient's vital signs.

~~age~~	anxiety	anger	caffeine	gender	humidity	infection
~~lifestyle~~	stress	temperature	tobacco			

Environmental	Social	Psychological	Physical
	lifestyle		*age*

Davina, 10 years   Rose, 53 years   Pilar, 47 years

Listening   **6**   🔵 **23**   At the shift change in ER, Staff Nurse Debbie updates her team. Listen.
Write the correct patient name on each chart a–c.

Chart a _____

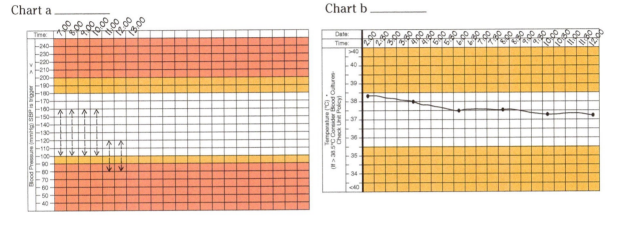

Chart b _____

Chart c _____

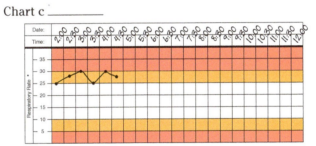

7   Listen again. Write D (Davina), P (Pilar), or R (Rose) next to each sentence.
Complete the sentences with the correct form of the words in the box.

and	down	stable	up	up and down	vary

1   Her Resps are still _____ .   _____
2   Her BP is _____ from 160 / 100 to 120 / 80.   _P_
3   Her Resps _____ between
    25 _____ 30.   _____
4   Her temperature was _____ to 38.2.   _____
5   Her temperature's _____ now.   _____

1   ↗   increase / rise / go up

2   ↘   decrease / fall / go down

3   ⌒   go up and down / vary between … and

4   —   be stable

5   ∧∧↗   go up and down

Vocabulary   **8**   Draw the correct arrow from 1–5 above next to each sentence in 7.

Taking vital signs

1 🎧 **24** Match the instructions 1–6 to the images a–f. Write the correct piece of equipment and the vital sign(s) next to each instruction. Then listen and repeat the instructions using the correct intonation pattern.

1 Could you just open your mouth for me, please?
2 Can you put your head on one side?
3 Can you just roll up your sleeve for me?
4 Can you give me your right hand, please?
5 Could you relax and breathe normally for me?
6 Could you hold your arm out straight?

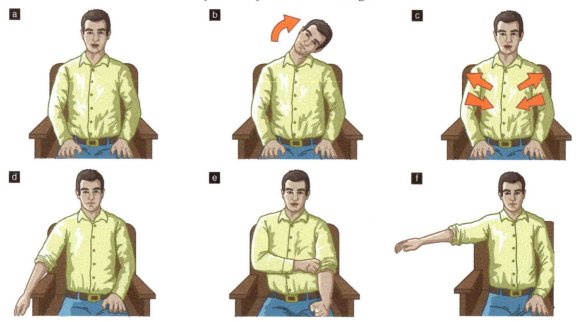

2 Charge Nurse Stefano takes Mr Daniels' pulse rate. Put the words in order to form sentences. Then put these sentences into the correct order 1–4.

a) give me / can you / your palm / please   _____
b) per minute / ninety-five beats / that's   _____
c) pulse now / if I can / Mr Daniels / I'll take your   _____
d) I'll put / your wrist / my fingers on   _____

3 🎧 **25** Listen and check. Why does the nurse need to take the patient's pulse twice?

4 🎧 **26** Stefano then takes Cameron's pulse. Listen and answer the questions. Work in pairs and compare your answers.

1 What method does the nurse use to take this patient's pulse?
2 What is the patient's pulse rate?
3 How old do you think the patient is? How do you know?

Language

Will + infinitive for future

We use **will** + infinitive to make predictions for the future and to talk about decisions.	Prediction: **You'll (you will)** *feel better soon.*
	Decision: **I'll (I will)** *take your temperature now.*

5 Complete these examples from Stefano's conversations with Mr Daniels and Cameron. Use *will* and the verbs in the box. Listen and check.

be	clip	hurt	put	take	write

1 I _____ my fingers on your wrist.
2 I _____ a second reading.
3 I _____ just _____ this little meter to your finger.
4 _____ it _____ ?
5 No, it _____ . It _____ very quick, I promise.
6 I _____ just _____ this down.

Listening 6 🔊 **27** Ana Leogardo, 32, is a patient on the Cardiology Ward. The staff nurse is doing her rounds before breakfast. Listen and answer these questions.

1 How does Ana feel?
2 How does the nurse take Ana's pulse?
3 How does the nurse feel about Ana's temperature?

7 Complete what the nurse says to Ana as she takes her blood pressure. Use *will* and the correct form of the verbs in the box.

be	eat	feel	hold	put	roll	see	take	wrap

I [1]_____ your sleeve up a little. That's good. We [2]_____ a pillow on your lap. Can you [3]_____ your arm out straight for me? You can rest it on the pillow. I [4]_____ the cuff round your arm. Just relax, that's right. You [5]_____ any pain; it [6]_____ a bit tight around your arm. OK? That's 130 / 85. I [7]_____ the cuff off now and then you can [8]_____ your breakfast in peace! I'll [9]_____ you later.

8 🔊 **28** Listen. Complete Ana's vital signs and check your answers to 7.

Patient name: *Ms Ana Leogardo*				Date of Birth: *22.07.79*	
BP	**P**	**RR**	**T**	**O$_2$ Sats**	**Signature**
				98%	*S. Renneke*

Writing 9 Choose one piece of equipment from 7 on page 21 and write five lines to explain how to take one of the vital signs. Then work in pairs and practise explaining to your partner.

Circulation and the heart

Vocabulary **1** Label the diagram of the heart with the words in the box.

1 *aorta*

2 _____

3 _____

4 _____

5 _____

6 _____

7 _____

8 _____

| aorta | left atrium | left ventricle | pulmonary artery | pulmonary vein |
| right atrium | right ventricle | vena cava | | |

Pronunciation **2** 🔊 **29** Which syllables are stressed? Underline the stressed syllables. Listen, check and repeat.

1 aorta
2 artery
3 vena cava
4 atrium
5 ventricle
6 pulmonary

Reading **3** Read and complete the information about the function of the heart. Use the words in the boxes.

WHAT THE DOES HEART DO?

The heart is a muscle that ¹_____ blood around the body. The blood ²_____ through to the other organs and takes food and oxygen to them. The blood then ³_____ to the heart via the veins.

| circulates | pumps | returns |

THE CHAMBERS OF THE HEART

Inside the heart there are four chambers. The two upper chambers are called the ⁴_____ . They receive and collect blood. The two lower chambers of the heart are called the ⁵_____ . They pump blood out of the heart into the ⁶_____ to other parts of the body.

| atria | circulatory system | ventricles |

THE BLOOD FLOW

Blood enters the right atrium of the heart from the superior and inferior ⁷_____ . The heart then pumps blood into the right ventricle. From there the blood goes into the lungs through the ⁸_____ , where it is filled with oxygen. The oxygen-rich blood then returns to the heart through the pulmonary veins into the left atrium. From there the blood is pumped into the left ventricle which then pumps it into the rest of the body through the ⁹_____ .

| aorta | pulmonary artery | vena cava |

Speaking **4** Work in pairs. Cover the text. Use the diagram and the words in the boxes to explain how the heart works.

Smoking and cardiovascular disease

Smoking is a major risk factor for getting cardiovascular (heart and blood vessel) disease. The more you smoke, the greater your risk. Did you know that nicotine and carbon monoxide from cigarettes have a significant effect on your heart and blood vessels? When you smoke, your heart rate increases and your blood pressure rises. At the same time, your arteries narrow and blood flow decreases.

Giving up smoking – what are the real benefits?

Your risk of heart disease begins to decrease almost immediately after you stop smoking.

In 20 minutes: your blood pressure and heart rate fall to their normal level.

In eight hours: your level of oxygen rises to its normal rate and your carbon dioxide level drops.

In 24 hours: your chance of a heart attack starts to go down.

In 12 months: your risk of a heart attack falls by more than 50%.

After several years: your risk of heart disease could be similar to that of someone who has never smoked at all.

Give up smoking – it's never too late!

Reading **5** Read the patient leaflet. Why is smoking bad for the heart?

6 Are these sentences *true* (T) or *false* (F)? Correct the false statements.
1 Your risk of cardiovascular disease is greater if you smoke. (T / F)
2 Nicotine will increase your blood flow and decrease your blood pressure. (T / F)
3 Heart rate returns to normal less than half an hour after stopping smoking. (T / F)
4 Even ex-smokers remain high risk for heart disease. (T / F)
5 It is sometimes too late to stop smoking. (T / F)

7 Cover the text. Complete a summary of the main points.
1 The risk of heart disease _____ the more you smoke.
2 Chemicals in cigarettes can block the arteries. The heart rate _____ and blood pressure _____ .
3 As soon as you stop smoking, the risk of heart disease _____ .
4 After eight hours, your oxygen level _____ and the level of carbon-dioxide _____ .
5 The risk of a heart attack _____ by 50 percent within 12 months.

Speaking **8** Work in pairs. You are going to advise a patient who is a heavy smoker. Take turns to play the role of the patient and the nurse. Follow these instructions.
1 Welcome your patient.
2 Explain the procedures for taking vital signs.
3 Take your patient's vital signs.
4 Explain the risks of smoking on the heart. (Use the correct stress pattern when pronouncing cardiology terms.)
5 Respond to your patient's questions about the benefits of giving up smoking.

- describe symptoms and injuries
- ask about symptoms and injuries
- give instructions in an asthma emergency
- talk about SOAP notes

Symptoms and injuries

Vocabulary **1** Complete the text about emergency rooms with the words in the box.

| abdominal | chest | contusion | injury | respiratory | sprain |

Why do people visit ER? The most common reason is for an [1]_____, in most cases a strain, [2]_____ or [3]_____. The second most common reason on the list is signs and symptoms of either [4]_____ or [5]_____ pain. People are also frequently brought into ER with [6]_____ problems.

2 Look at the patients a–f in the Emergency Room and discuss.

1 Why do you think each patient has come to the Emergency Room? What health problems do they have?
2 Which order do you think the triage nurse should see the patients?

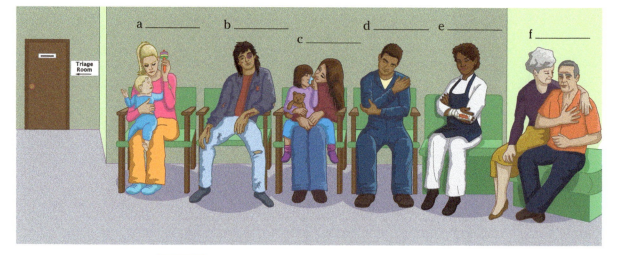

a_____   b_____   d_____   e_____   f_____
c_____

Listening **3** 🔊 **30** Listen to the six patients describing their problems. Label the pictures a–f in the order you hear them 1–6.

4 Listen again and write the description of the problem next to the person.

| asthma | black eye | bleeding | broken wrist | colic |
| contusion | heart problem | infection | nausea | |

5 Complete the sentences about the patients' injuries and symptoms with the correct form of the words in the box.

| bleed breathe bruise cough dizzy (x2) infect pain (x2) sickness swell |

1 Aisha is _____ a lot and having difficulty _____ .
2 Sandip has _____ in his chest and feels _____ .
3 Desiree is _____ heavily from a bad cut and is worried about _____ .
4 Jasmine has a bad stomach _____ . Twice I gave her milk, but she was _____ almost immediately.
5 Winston' shoulder and wrist are very _____ and painful. He banged his head hard and still feels _____ and nauseous.
6 Jason fell off his bike and has cuts and _____ on his right arm.

6 Complete the table with the correct word forms. Which nouns are synonyms for more formal medical words?

Noun	Verb	Adjective
blood	to [1]_____	bloody
breathlessness	to be short of breath	[2]_____
[3]_____	to bruise	bruised
cough	to [4]_____	
dizziness		[5]_____
infection	to [6]_____	infected
[7]_____		painful
swelling	to [8]_____	swollen
sickness	to feel / to be [9]_____	

Language

Past simple v past continuous	
We use the **past simple** tense to talk about finished actions in the past.	I **started** taking gentle exercise and my asthma symptoms **improved**.
We use the **past continuous** to talk about continuous or uninterrupted actions in the past.	You **were coughing** all night – I heard you.

7 Complete the sentences with the correct form of the verb in brackets.

1 My son _____ (play) soccer in the park with his dad and he _____ (fall over) and _____ (pull) a muscle in his leg.
2 My wife _____ (cough) all night so I _____ (phone) the medical helpline. They _____ (tell) me to make an appointment with her GP.
3 Kira _____ (run) a high temperature when the ambulance services _____ (bring) her in.
4 My headaches _____ (not / stop) immediately. The tablets I _____ (take) _____ (no / be) strong enough.
5 The patient _____ (present) to ER at 11pm. He _____ (suffer) from serious vomiting.
6 Can you tell me what you _____ (do) when your asthma attack _____ (start)?
7 My father _____ (have) difficulties walking and he _____ (trip) and _____ (fall) in the street.
8 I _____ (not think) and I _____ (give) him the wrong dose of aspirin. He's only three. What should I do? I'm really worried.

Asking about symptoms and injuries

Speaking

1 Look at the patient in this photo. Work in pairs and discuss these questions.

1 What are the patient's symptoms?
2 What do you think the patient is suffering from?
3 What do you think he was doing when his problem started?

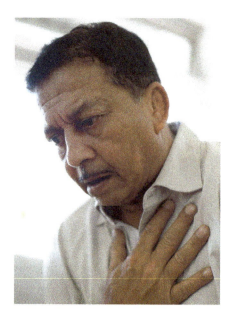

Listening

2 🎧 **31** Listen to the nurse interviewing Mr Daniels and check your answers in 1.

3 Listen again and complete the patient record.

---

med*TRUST* ❤️ hospital

Patient Record

Mr Daniels is 54. He has pains in the [1]_____ and is suffering from [2]_____ of breath. The pain is located in the [3]_____ of the chest and radiates down his left [4]_____ and up into his [5]_____ . The pain usually lasts for around [6]_____ minutes.

The pain began when he [7]_____ at his work place. The patient works in a supermarket. The patient has suffered from the attacks for [8]_____ months. This is his [9]_____ attack. He is also suffering from problems with his [10]_____ .

The pain improves when he takes painkillers. He is [11]_____ about his condition.

He thinks stress makes his condition [12]_____ .

Vocabulary

4 Match the beginnings 1–8 and the endings a–h to complete the nurse's questions.

1 How would you describe	a)	how bad was the pain?
2 Can you	b)	move at all?
3 On a scale of one to ten,	c)	me how it started?
4 Does the pain	d)	the pain in your chest?
5 How long	e)	makes it worse?
6 Can you tell	f)	about your condition, Mr Daniels?
7 Anything that	g)	explain where exactly?
8 How do you feel	h)	did the pain last this time?

5 Turn to audio script 31 on page 74 to read all the nurse's questions and check your answers in 4. Answer these questions.

1 Circle all the closed questions (questions with only one possible answer). Underline all the open questions (questions that invite the patient to express their own ideas).
2 What are the advantage and disadvantages of asking open questions?
3 What are the advantages and disadvantages of asking closed questions?

6 Decide if these questions are Open (O) or Closed (C). Imagine the situation and write a possible answer for each question

1 How are you feeling this morning?   _O_
2 What happens when you get angina?   _____
3 When did James start feeling ill?   _____
4 Does it hurt when I press your abdomen just here?   _____
5 How bad is the pain?   _____
6 Tell me, what were you doing when the symptoms appeared?   _____
7 Were you taking your medication?   _____
8 Can you describe the symptoms to me?   _____
9 Tell me how it happened.   _____
10 Are you still in pain?   _____

7 Compare your answers with a partner. Which questions do you think are more useful in a nurse to patient situation?

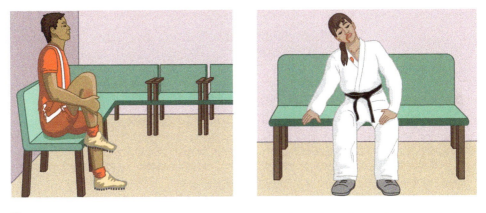

8 These patients have common sports injuries. Complete the dialogues with the nurse treating them in ER. Use the question forms from 4 and 6 to help you.

1
Nurse: Can you tell me [1]_____ ?
Ahmed: I don't know. I was playing really well and then [2]_____ .
Nurse: How many times [3]_____ ?
Ahmed: This is the first time.
Nurse: Does it hurt when [4]_____ ?
Ahmed: Arrgh, yes, it's [5]_____ .
Nurse: On a scale [6]_____ ?
Ahmed: [7]_____ .

2
Nurse: Ooo, that looks painful. Tell me [8]_____ .
Vicky: [9]_____ .
Nurse: Do you have any other symptoms?
Vicky: I'm not sure. What do you mean?
Nurse: [10]_____ , for example.
Vicky: [11]_____ .

Speaking **9** 🔊 **32** Listen and check. Did you ask the same questions? Work in pairs and practise the dialogues.

Asthma emergency – giving instructions

Speaking   **1**   You are going to read some information from the WHO (World Health Organization) about asthma. What are the symptoms and causes of asthma? Work in pairs and discuss.

Vocabulary   **2**   Match the words 1–6 with the definitions a–f.

1	breathless	a)	to make part of the body feel sore
2	irritate	b)	a fine powder produced by flowers
3	mucus	c)	having problems breathing
4	pollen	d)	to stop the feeling of pain
5	relieve	e)	to breathe noisily and with difficulty
6	wheeze	f)	a thick liquid produced in parts of the body

Reading   **3**   Read the text and check your answers to 1. Label the diagram with the words in the box.

asthmatic bronchiole	bronchial tubes	diaphragm	left lung
normal bronchiole	right lung	windpipe	

Asthma — a global problem

Asthma is a chronic respiratory disease. The symptoms are a 'tight', chest, coughing, wheezing and difficulty in breathing. When a person with asthma comes into contact with something that irritates their airways, the lining of the bronchial tubes starts to swell. This makes the airways narrower and it is more difficult for air to get in and out of the lungs. Sometimes mucus is also produced. All of these cause the patient to wheeze, cough and become breathless.

- Asthma is the most common chronic disease among children.
- Asthma is a major public health problem for many countries in the world.
- The country with the highest level of asthma is the United Kingdom, followed by New Zealand.
- Over 80% of asthma deaths happen in low and lower-middle income countries.
- The causes of asthma are not completely understood. It is hereditary (it runs in family and is passed from parent to child) and is linked with allergies. Things that cause allergic reactions include:

  □ indoor allergens (e.g. dust, pet hair)   □ chemicals in the workplace

  □ outdoor allergens (e.g. pollens)   □ air pollution.

  □ tobacco smoke

Although there is no cure for asthma, it is possible to control the symptoms and enjoy a good quality of life.

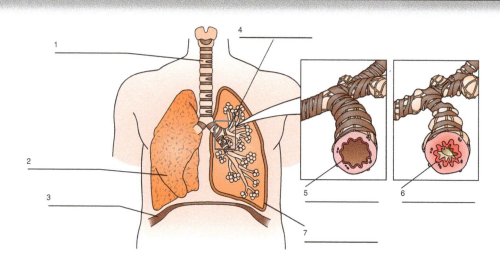

Listening **4** 🔊 33 Kyle Jenkins is attending an asthma clinic run by Nina, a practice nurse. Listen to the dialogue. Are these sentences *true* (T) or *false* (F)? Correct the false sentences.

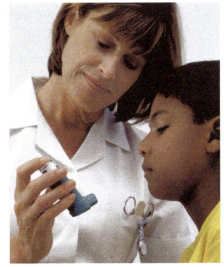

1 The patient has suffered two asthma attacks this week.
2 The patient was playing tennis with his cousin when he had the last attack.
3 The patient's attack lasted about ten minutes.
4 The patient's best friend is also asthmatic.
5 The patient is going to practise how to use his inhaler correctly.

5 Put these words in order to form sentences. Then put sentences a–e in order 1–5 to form a set of instructions for using an inhaler.

a) don't breathe / on your / Take a puff / inhaler at the same time / but / out immediately ____
b) your breath / the inhaler / Remove / for 10 seconds / hold / and ____
c) the mouthpiece / as possible / as deeply / Place / breathe in / and / between your lips ____
d) if necessary / Breathe / and / repeat / out slowly ____
e) back slightly / tilt your head / gently / and / Breathe out ___1___

Language

The imperative	
We use **imperatives** to give clear, simple instructions to a patient.	***Take*** *your time.* ***Don't*** *lie down.*
We can use **staging words**, e.g. *first, then, next, finally* followed by a short pause to make it easier for the patient to understand the instructions.	***First***, *breathe out.* ***Then***, *blow into the mouthpiece.*

6 Use the verbs in the box to complete the instructions the practice nurse gives Kyle in an emergency.

call	continue	lean	lie down	put	repeat	sit	take

1_____ down at a table. Don't 2_____ . 3_____ forward slightly and 4_____ your arms on the table.
5_____ up to six puffs of your inhaler.
6_____ an ambulance after six minutes if your symptoms don't improve.
7_____ to take your inhaler every six minutes, for a maximum of six puffs.
8_____ these steps, if your symptoms begin again.

Speaking **7** 🔊 34 Rewrite the instructions in 6 to include staging words. Work in pairs and take turns to practise reading them aloud. Pause slightly after each staging word. Then listen and check.

SOAP notes

Patient Name:	Kyle Jenkins
DOB:	06.04.2001
Record No:	TT-5810 fl133
Subjective:	'My chest feels all tight.'
Objective:	RR 28, wheezing, SOB, abdominal exertion
Assessment:	breathing pattern r/t asthma
Plan:	1) position pt in High Fowlers
	2) administer meds via nebulizer

Reading **1** Look at the SOAP note that Nina wrote about Kyle. Then read the text about SOAP notes. Complete the text with the words in the box.

documents	help	measure	summary	symptoms	treat

SOAP notes are [1]_____ that nurses use to record information about a patient. A SOAP note has four parts – Subjective, Objective, Assessment and Plan.

The Subjective is what the patient says about his or her problem. It is the [2]_____ the patient (or the patient's family) describes.

The Objective is what the nurse sees or observes at the time. It is the symptoms that the nurse can see, feel, hear, touch and [3]_____ .

The Assessment is the nurse's [4]_____ of what the patient's immediate medical problems are.

The Plan is what the nurse plans to do to [5]_____ the patient's symptoms and [6]_____ with the problem.

Vocabulary **2** Read Kyle's SOAP note again and find the expressions or abbreviations in the note which mean the following.

1 medicine or medication
2 patient
3 related to
4 short of breath
5 his abdomen is working hard because he is having problems breathing
6 give
7 respiratory rate
8 a piece of equipment that administers medication that the patient breaths in

Speaking **3** What is High Fowler's? How does High Fowler's help an asthmatic patient? Explain how to position a patient into the High Fowler's position.

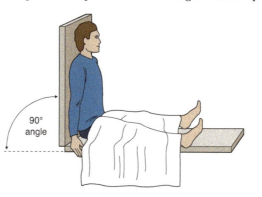

90°
angle

4 Look at the SOAP notes for the two patients below and answer these questions.

Who …

1 … suffers from arthritis?
2 … would like to lose weight?
3 … will see their old school friends a year from now?
4 … will have their next appointment in three months?
5 … doesn't suffer from drug allergies?
6 … has to write down their feelings in a diary as part of their treatment?

Patient Name: Nancy Suzman
DOB: 14.10.62
Record No. FM–967–PPK

S 'I've a been overweight since the birth of my twin daughters in 2001 and I get frustrated trying to diet. My 25-year reunion is next year and I'd really like to lose some weight.' NKDA, NKA.

O Wt = 95 kg Ht = 1m 60 IBW = 115 kg Chol = 255 BP = 120 / 75

A Obese at 183% IBW, hypercholesterolemia

P Long Term Goal: Change lifestyle habits to lose at least 27 kg over a 10-month period.

Short Term Goal: Client to begin a 1500 calorie diet with walking 30 minutes per day.

Instructed Pt on lower fat food choices and smaller food portions.

Client will keep a daily food and mood record to review next session.

Follow-up in one week.

Signature: *Nina Farrer*

Patient Name: Massimo Geraldo
DOB: 17.05.1957
Record No. YF- 556-UIi68

S 'I've had this pain in my right knee for four months; its worse when I walk or do any exercise.' NKDA.

O Wt. 69 kg, Ht.1m 67, normal ROM both knees no redness or swelling

A Possible osteoarthritis; R/O rheumatoid arthritis

P (1) blood work–sed rate rheumatoid factor
(2) X-ray R knee PA and lateral
(3) ibuprofen 400 mg t.i.d. p.o.
(4) recheck in 3 months.

Signature: *Nina Farrer*

Abbreviations key:

IBW = ideal body weight	BS = blood sugar	b. i. d. = twice a day
Chol = cholesterol	UA = urine analysis	ABC = airways, breathing, circulation
ROM = range of motion	R = right	IBP = ineffective breathing pattern
R/O = rule out	L = left	
PA = posterior/anterior	mg = milligram	O^2 = oxygen
NKDA = no known drug allergies	t.i.d. = three times a day	p.r.n. = as required
NKA = no known allergies	p.o. = by mouth	hr = hour
	IAC = ineffective airway clearance	

5 Work in pairs. Practise saying these abbreviations as complete words.

6 Work in pairs. Student A, look at the information below. Student B, turn to page 68.

sed rate: a blood test that can show inflammatory activity in the body

Dictate the nursing terms to your partner, who will write the abbreviation. Add two more of your own examples. When you have finished, swap roles.

1 by mouth
2 cholesterol
3 rule out
4 milligram
5 no known allergies
6 ineffective airway clearance
7 ideal body weight
8 urine analysis

5

Food and nutrition

- talk about food and nutrition
- assess nutritional status
- talk about food allergies and intolerances
- offer advice on diet

Nutrition

Level 4
(0–3 servings)

Level 3
(2–3 servings)

Level 2
(2–4 fruit / 3–5 vegetables)

Level 1
(6–11 servings)

1 _____

2 _____

3 _____

4 _____

Vocabulary

1 Look at the food pyramid for a healthy diet. Label sections 1–4 with the words from column 3 in the table below. Compare your answers in pairs.

2 Look at the food groups table. Complete the gaps in column 2 with the words in the box.

| bones | build | digest | energy | fight | repair | skin |

Food group	What do they do for your body?	Where can you find them?
carbohydrates	They give you [1]_____ .	potatoes, rice, cereal, pasta, bread
fats	They also give energy and help [2]_____ the body.	dairy products, meat, oils, sweets
fibre	It helps you to [3]_____ your food.	
minerals	Calcium is good for your [4]_____ . Iron is good for the blood. Zinc helps you [5]_____ infection.	fresh fruit and vegetables (zinc in seafood)
proteins	They help the body grow and [6]_____ itself.	meat, fish, dairy products, beans, eggs
vitamins A, B, C, D and E	Vitamins are necessary for your [7]_____ , bones and teeth.	fresh fruit and vegetables, dairy products

Language

Countable and uncountable nouns	
Countable nouns can be singular or plural.	*a biscuit, three biscuits, an egg, two eggs*
Uncountable nouns only exist as 'mass'.	*(water) some water, (sugar) some sugar*
NB water; cheese = uncountable a bottle of water, piece of cheese = countable	
We use **a lot of** for countable and uncountable nouns.	***a lot of** cheese, eggs, biscuits*
In questions and negatives, use **many** for countable, **much** for uncountable nouns.	*How **many** eggs? Not **many**.*
	*How **much** water? Not **much**.*

3 Complete the table with as many examples as possible from the food pyramid.

Countable nouns	Uncountable nouns
an apple, two apples, a piece of cheese	*some fruit, some cheese*

4 Look at the photos of the four women from different parts of the world and read the texts. Match the people a–d with their diets 1–4.

1 I'm ¹ *a/an* Muslim so I don't eat ² *some/any* pork dishes, but I do eat ³ *a lot/not a lot* of chicken. We have wonderful desserts in Morocco, but there's often too ⁴ *much/many* honey for me and they're really sweet, so I don't eat ⁵ *a lot of/a little of* them. I prefer eating vegetables and salads.

2 As ¹ *a/an* diabetic I don't eat ² *much/many* meat and I also don't eat too ³ *many/much* dairy products. What I really like is chocolate, but I have to be careful. Sometimes I have ⁴ *a/an/some* bar of chocolate as a special treat. Last week was my birthday and my grandchildren bought me ⁵ *a/an/some* Belgian chocolates, which were delicious.

3 My children are quite fussy and I generally don't cook ¹ *any/some* food that they don't like. We don't eat ² *any/some* shellfish, but we do eat fish – I had ³ *some/a/an* salmon for lunch today which was really tasty. I enjoy making vegetarian sushi. I also cook with ⁴ *a lot of/not any* grains and tofu for the protein.

4 I'm ¹ *a/an* Australian-born Indian. My husband was born in India and usually cooks traditional food, but personally I don't like too ² *many/much* spicy food. We don't eat ³ *any/some* products made of beef, so we never eat ⁴ *any/some* fast food, as we're never sure what it contains. But my favourite is fruit. I eat quite ⁵ *a lot/not any* of it, especially tropical fruit, like papaya and pineapple, which I love.

5 Read the texts in 4 again and underline the best word in each case.

Writing **6** Write a short paragraph to describe your own diet and eating habits.

Nutritional status

Vocabulary **1** Read about how to calculate BMI or body mass index. Complete the gaps with the words in the box.

obese	overweight	underweight

BMI

Body mass index or BMI is used to decide if a person's weight is healthy or not.

To calculate a person's BMI, we use the formula:

$$\frac{\text{Weight in kilograms}}{\text{Height in metres}^2}$$

Readings

BMI of less than 18.5 is [1]_____

BMI from 18.5 to 24.9 is the right weight for women

BMI from 20.5 to 25.0 is the right weight for men

BMI of 25 to 29.9 is [2]_____

BMI of 30 is [3]_____

Listening **2** 🔊 **35** You are going to hear Nurse Sam McCarthy assessing Alain. As you listen, complete the Nursing Assessment form.

Diet restrictions and requirements	Yes	No	If YES _____ _____
	☐	☐	
a) BMI _____			
b) Food allergies	Yes ☑	No ☐	If YES _____
c) Last meal (date / time) _____	Give details _____ _____		

3 Underline the correct information in these statements.

1 The patient's BMI indicates he is *slightly overweight / slightly underweight*.
2 The patient wants to *gain weight / lose weight*.
3 The patient's *current weight / normal weight* is seventy-five kilos.
4 The patient *overeats / doesn't eat enough*.

Food Journal: *Alain Sunderland*		
Tuesday	**Time**	**Typical Food Intake**
Breakfast	7.00	nothing
Mid morning	10.30	coffee
Lunch	12.30	chicken + tomato sandwich (brown bread), coffee
Mid afternoon	15.00	one small apple
Dinner	19.00	nothing
Evening	22.00+	cup of vegetable soup (packet), two slices brown toast, carbonated drink, coffee

Speaking **4** Work in pairs. Look at Alain's food journal and discuss.

1 What is good and bad about Alain's diet?
2 What advice would you give him about his weight?

5 🔘 **36** You are going to hear Nurse Sam assessing Alain's food intake. Compare her assessment of his diet with yours.

6 Complete the sentences using the words in the box. Listen again and check.

balanced	energy	intake	lack	skipping	snack	source

1 Your calorie _____ is very low.
2 It's not a _____ diet.
3 You _____ protein, carbohydrates and fibre.
4 You're _____ breakfast.
5 After eight to ten hours without food, your body needs _____ .
6 Brown bread is a good _____ of fibre.
7 The only _____ you took yesterday was a piece of fruit.

7 🔘 **37** Listen to the final part and complete the assessment.

Mr Sunderland is a _____ . He could bring _____ to work.

Reading **8** Read Annabelle Driver's case history and her food journal. Write six sentences assessing her food intake. Write about these things.

1 her calorie intake
2 how balanced her diet is
3 snacks
4 meals that she skips
5 fibre
6 what she should eat more of

Case History: Ms Annabelle Driver, 34, is recovering from varicose vein surgery. The patient is unemployed and a single parent with two teenagers living in a deprived area. She suffers from asthma and has a BMI of 30. Because of her weight, the patient finds it difficult to exercise. Ms Driver has also suffered from mild depression in the past.

Food Journal: *Annabelle Driver*

Tuesday	Time	Typical Food Intake
Breakfast	9.00	nothing
Mid morning	11.00	large milky coffee and 2–3 biscuits
Lunch	13.30	two burgers, large portion of chips, two bananas, packet of nuts, two cokes
Mid afternoon	15.00	two cups of tea, large packet of crisps, one doughnut
Tea	17.00	a banana, a chocolate bar
Dinner	20.00	large serving of pasta, meat sauce, ice-cream, cake, an apple, two cokes
Evening	23.30	cup of tea and 5–6 biscuits

Speaking **9** Write your own food journal. Prepare to present an assessment of your food intake to the class. Use the same headings as for Annabelle Driver in 8.

Food allergies and intolerances

Speaking **1** Which foods are people often allergic to? What are the symptoms of an allergy? Work in pairs and discuss.

Reading **2** Match the words with the definitions.

1	adverse	a)	it protects the body from infection
2	immune system	b)	substances that destroy disease
3	harmful	c)	negative or bad
4	antibodies	d)	it can hurt you

3 Complete the first part of the patient leaflet with words from 2 above.

What is a food allergy?

If you experience an [1] _____ reaction to a food, this is sometimes because of a food allergy. A food allergy occurs when the [2] _____ believes, by mistake, that a food is [3] _____ . When this happens, the immune system creates special [4] _____ to help it protect the body from the harmful food. The next time you eat that food, these antibodies go to work. They tell the immune system to release chemicals called histamines into the body. These chemicals cause the allergic symptoms which can affect your respiratory system, gastrointestinal tract, skin or cardiovascular system. A strong allergic reaction can kill you.

---

4 Read the second part of the patient leaflet and check your answers to 1.

Causes and symptoms

Any food can cause an allergic reaction. However, 90% of all reactions are caused by the following eight foods: fish and shellfish, peanuts, milk, eggs, wheat, nuts and soy.

Food allergy symptoms generally appear within a few minutes or up to two hours after eating one of these foods. Symptoms include minor reactions such as a tingling sensation in the mouth, a rash and swelling, or eczema, abdominal cramps, diarrhoea, or vomiting. More serious reactions could be swelling of the tongue and throat, wheezing, breathing difficulties, or a decrease in blood pressure. Loss of consciousness is also possible and even death, although this is very rare.

If you have any of these symptoms after eating, tell your doctor, even if the symptoms are mild or disappear within a few minutes.

Pronunciation **5** Work in pairs. Take turns to read the sentences out loud. Underline the stressed syllable in the words in bold.

1 My son has lots of food **allergies**.
2 She has a severe **allergic** reaction to nuts.
3 I had a pain in my **abdomen**.
4 Do you suffer from **abdominal** pain?
5 His **respiratory** system was affected.
6 **Respiration** is one of the vital signs.

6 🔊 38 Listen and check your answers. Then listen again and repeat.

Speaking **7** What do you know about diabetes? Work in pairs and discuss these questions.

1 What is diabetes?
2 What causes diabetes?
3 What are the treatments for diabetes?

Reading **8** Read this definition of diabetes from a nursing reference book and check your answers in 7.

Diabetes

Diabetes mellitus (sometimes called sugar diabetes) is a condition that occurs when the body can't process glucose properly and has very high blood sugar. Glucose is sugar that the body uses for energy and it is normally controlled by a hormone called insulin. Insulin is produced by the pancreas and if a person has diabetes this is either because the pancreas does not make enough insulin (Type 1 diabetes) or the body can't respond normally to the insulin that is made (Type 2 diabetes). A level of blood sugar produces the classic diabetes symptoms of needing to urinate very often, feeling thirsty and losing weight. However, it is very common for overweight people to get diabetes so the condition is linked to obesity. Patients with Type 1 diabetes can control the condition with insulin and patients with Type 2 diabetes can control it with diet and exercise.

Listening **9** 🔊 39 Listen to Joely Thomas, a student nurse, learning how to administer a blood sugar test. Label the diagram with the words in the box.

blood glucose chart   drop of blood   finger   glucometer   lancet   plaster   screen   test strip

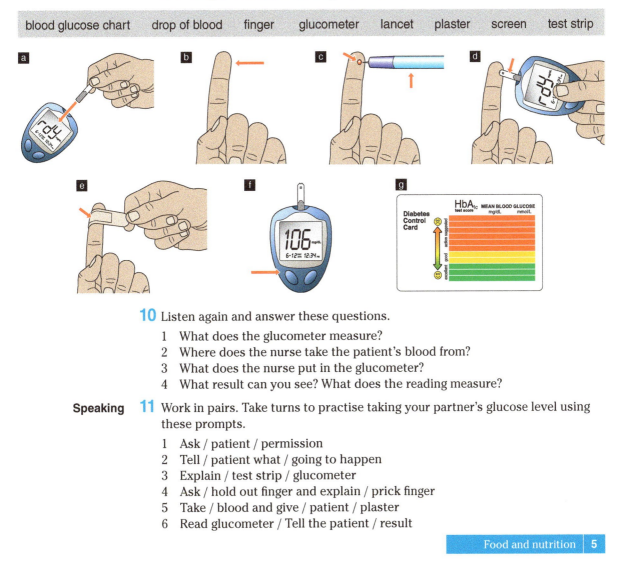

10 Listen again and answer these questions.

1 What does the glucometer measure?
2 Where does the nurse take the patient's blood from?
3 What does the nurse put in the glucometer?
4 What result can you see? What does the reading measure?

Speaking **11** Work in pairs. Take turns to practise taking your partner's glucose level using these prompts.

1 Ask / patient / permission
2 Tell / patient what / going to happen
3 Explain / test strip / glucometer
4 Ask / hold out finger and explain / prick finger
5 Take / blood and give / patient / plaster
6 Read glucometer / Tell the patient / result

Advice on diet

1 _____
2 _____
3 _____
4 _____
5 _____

6 _____
7 _____
8 _____
9 _____
10 _____

Vocabulary **1** Label the pictures with the words in the box.

> bottle   can   carton   glass   packet   piece   segment   slice   stick   tablespoon

Listening **2** 🎧 **40** Listen to Maggie, a school nurse, giving advice about nutrition to a group of adolescents. As you listen, tick (✓) the quantities you hear.

☐ a lot of   ☐ carton   ☐ portion   ☐ segment   ☐ not many
☐ packet   ☐ slice   ☐ can   ☐ stick

3 Listen again and answer the questions.

1 What advice does the government give?
2 What is a portion of fruit? *(two examples)*
3 What is a portion of vegetables? *(two examples)*
4 What does Maggie say about starchy vegetables such as potatoes?
5 What is Maggie's advice about ready-meals?

4 🎧 **41** You're going to hear practice nurse Brad Tyler giving advice to three of his patients. Listen and complete the statement for each patient.

1 Lena is recovering from glandular fever and wants to _____ .
2 Frank has just had a heart attack and wants to _____ .
3 Edith is on a weight loss programme, but she needs to _____ .

5 Listen again and complete the nurse's suggestions. Then match each one to the correct patient L (Lena), F (Frank) or E (Edith).

_____ 1 How about _____ the _____ ?
_____ 2 Can I suggest you _____ little and _____ at first.
_____ 3 Why don't you try _____ _____ instead of meat?
_____ 4 It is important to _____ if you want to _____ _____ .
_____ 5 And it's important to _____ lots of _____ .

Language

Giving suggestions and advice	
should / ***shouldn't*** + infinitive	*You **should** eat more fruit and vegetables.*
	*You **shouldn't** eat fatty foods.*
tentative suggestions	***How about drinking** more water?*
	***Can I suggest you** try a vegan diet?*
strong suggestions	*It is **advisable to** give up smoking if you are pregnant.*
	*It is **important to** eat more fibre.*

6 Rewrite these suggestions replacing *should* with another expression from the box.

Example: *1 It's advisable to only eat red meat once a month, according to government advice.*

1 You should only eat red meat once a month, according to government advice.
2 You shouldn't skip breakfast; it's the most important meal of the day.
3 You should play football with your kids in the park.
4 You shouldn't have more than one cup of coffee a night.
5 You should go swimming if this is your favourite sport.
6 You shouldn't include too many complex carbohydrates in your diet.

Writing **7** Write two pieces of advice each for Lena, Frank and Edith.

Speaking **8** Work in pairs. Student A, look at the information below, Student B, turn to page 68.

1 You are Susie Marshall and Student B is your doctor. Talk about your diet and answer the doctor's questions. Listen to their advice on how you can improve your diet.
2 You are Student B's doctor. Find out about their diet. Ask questions and make notes. Offer advice on how they can improve their diet.

Case history:

Susie Marshall, 30 years, is single and works as a financial advisor. She trains at her local gym for 60 minutes a day. She is in a stressful job and sometimes suffers from dizziness, but has no other symptoms. Her GP has asked you to give Susie advice on a diet plan. Susie has been vegetarian since she was at university.

Food Journal: *Susie Marshall*	**BMI:** *18.9*	
Tuesday	**Time**	**Typical Food Intake**
Breakfast	*7.00*	*nothing*
Mid morning	*10.30*	*apple, carton yogurt*
Lunch	*12.30*	*cheese sandwich*
Mid afternoon	*15.00*	*small carton apple juice*
Dinner	*19.00*	*salad, ½ baked potato, carbonated drink*
Evening	*20.00+*	*cup of coffee*

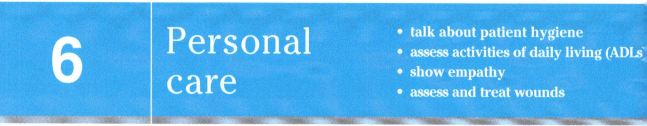

6

Personal care

• talk about patient hygiene
• assess activities of daily living (ADLs
• show empathy
• assess and treat wounds

Patient hygiene

Vocabulary

1 The charge nurse is going to help two patients with washing and grooming. Label the objects with the words in the box.

blanket	brush	comb	deodorant	disposable wipes	dressing gown
hand cream	kidney basin	make-up	mirror	nail brush	nightdress
pyjamas	razor	shampoo	shaving cream	soap	swab	toothbrush
toothpaste	towel	washbowl	washcloth

2 Put the objects in the correct column in the table. Some items may go in more than one column.

Washing	Grooming	Oral Hygiene	Patient Clothing
washbowl *blanket*	*nail brush*	*toothpaste*	*nightdress*

Listening **3** 🎧 **42** Listen as the nurse helps two patients with their washing and grooming. Are these statements *true* (T) or *false* (F)? Correct the false statements.

1 Mrs Turner is totally independent. (T / F)
2 Mary is breathless today. (T / F)
3 Mrs Turner needs help brushing her teeth. (T / F)
4 Mary needs more help than usual today. (T / F)
5 Mrs Turner gets tired quickly. (T / F)
6 The nurse tries to rush (hurry) the patients. (T / F)
7 The nurse encourages the patient to be independent. (T / F)

4 Which pieces of equipment does the nurse use to help Mrs Turner and Mary? Tick (✓) the correct columns in the table.

	hairbrush	kidney basin	mirror	soap	swab	towel	washcloth
Mrs Turner							
Mary							

Language

Be going to + infinitive for future	
Use **be going to** + infinitive to talk about your intentions and events that are planned or scheduled.	**I'm going to** explain the procedure to you first.
	We're going to help you take a shower.
	Are you going to help Mrs Hope with her hair?

5 Read the situations. What do you think the nurse or doctor intends to do? Complete the sentences and questions with the correct form of *be going to* and the verbs in the box.

check	explain	help	not discharge	not give	take

1 Mrs Taylor wants to take a shower.
This is Nurse Nandi. She _____ you get ready to go to the shower room.
2 Charlie Baker is finishing his lunch.
I _____ Charlie a bed bath at the moment. He's still eating.
3 Mary went to the bathroom an hour ago.
_____ you _____ on Mary? I'm a bit worried, she's still in the toilets.
4 The doctor doesn't think Mr Wang is well enough to leave the hospital.
Dr Charlton _____ Mr Wang this morning.
5 Mr Jones is worried about what's going to happen when he goes for therapy.
We _____ the procedure as we go along. If you have any questions, please just ask us.
6 Suzie needs help to wash her hair.
_____ you _____ Suzie some hot water? She's waiting for you.

Writing **6** Write three questions you could ask a patient in the future, using *be going to*. Work in pairs and compare your ideas.

Example: *1   What is the first thing you are going to eat after surgery?*

1 What …
2 Who are you going to …
3 When …
4 How …

ADLs – activities of daily living

Vocabulary **1** Label the pictures with the words in the box. What are the main ADLs? Which ADLs would this equipment help patients with?

| bed pan | commode | shower chair | urinal bottle |
| walker / walking frame | | walking stick | |

_____ _____ _____ _____

Listening **2** 🔊 **43** Listen and complete the ADL assessment for patients 1–4 in the table. Write *independent, needs help,* or *dependent* for each ADL.

ADLs	1 Mr Karam	2 Elaine	3 Samson	4 Mr Bates
washing	*independent*			
dressing				
grooming				
oral hygiene				
toileting				

Language

-ing form
We use the **-ing** form of the verb:

after certain verbs – e.g. *like, love, hate, begin, start, stop, finish,* etc.	*He **hates** using the commode.*
	*She **finished** dressing the patient.*
after prepositions – e.g. *with, without,* etc.	*Do you need help **with** washing?*
	*I can't put on my shoes **without** bending down.*

3 Listen again and answer the questions. Use the *-ing* form in your answers.
1 Why does Mr Karam have problems with shaving?
  Because his hands are shaky …
2 Why is it difficult for Elaine to put her tights on by herself?
  Because her back hurts and …
3 What else does Elaine need help with?
  She needs a hand with …
4 What doesn't Samson want help with?
5 What doesn't Mr Bates need help with and what does he hate using?

4 Put the words in order to form sentences. Write *Offer*, *Request*, or *Refusal of help* next to each one.

Offer   1   What / need help / do you / Elaine? / with,

_____   2   need / anything else? / Do you / help with

_____   3   Could you / with / give me a hand / washing my hair?

_____   4   cleaning your teeth? / need help / Do you / with

_____   5   everything by myself / try to do / today. / I want to

_____   6   getting to the toilet. / Can you / I need help / help me?

Speaking   **5**   Work in pairs. Write three short dialogues based on the following scenarios. Remember to use the *-ing* form. Practise reading them aloud.

1   Mrs Carter is very independent. The nurse offers to help with dressing and washing, but Mrs Carter wants to do everything by herself. She asks the nurse to fetch her walking frame so she can get to the bathroom.

2   Jared asks the nurse for help with shaving; his hands are shaking after his operation. The nurse offers to help him take a shower, but he refuses; he wants to do it by himself. He asks her for a shower chair.

3   The nurse brings Mr Onarian the urinal bottle, but he tells her that he hates using it. He asks her to help him get to the toilet.

6   Work with a different partner. Student A, use the information below. Student B, turn to page 69. Student A begins by taking the role of nurse. Ask Student B questions to complete the ADLs checklist 1. When you have finished, exchange roles. Use the notes in checklist 2 to reply to Student B's questions.

1

ADL Checklist

Patient Name: *Miles Denis*   **Ward:** *2*

Function	Independent	Needs Help	Dependent
Bathing / Showering			
Dressing			
Grooming			
Oral Hygiene			
Toileting			

2

ADL Checklist

Patient Name: *Sophie Mellors*   **Ward:** *1*

Function	Independent	Needs Help	Dependent
Bathing / Showering		*uses shower chair help washing hair*	
Dressing		*help with some items of clothing*	
Grooming	*has all her own toiletries*		
Oral Hygiene	*uses stick to access bathroom*		
Toileting	*uses stick to access bathroom*		

Empathy

Reading **1** Read Sections 1 and 2 of the complaint form and answer these questions.

    1 What do you learn about the patient?
    2 What do you think the complaint is about?

University Hospital Patient Relations Department	**COMPLAINT FORM**
[Section 1] **Patient's name:** *Mr Winston Miller* **Age:** *88* yrs **Ethnicity of patient:** *Afro Caribbean* **Name of person making complaint:** *Ms Deidre Hynd (daughter)* **Dept:** *Geriatrics* **Consultant of patient:** *Dr Hew Jones*	**[Section 2]** **Date of event(s):** *15.05.10 to 20.05.10* **Location of event(s):** *St Marc's Ward*

[Section 3]
Please provide an account of the incident(s) leading to the complaint being made:
My father suffers from early dementia and requires assistance with simple tasks. In general the staff are kind and helpful, but he often complains about Nurse Jones. This nurse is often too busy to help my father and sometimes refuses to help him to eat. According to my father, Nurse Jones is very impolite, treats him like a child and complains about him to other patients. Quote 'I'm not paid enough to clean up after stupid, old men like Winston.' I visited my father on 19 May at 10.30am. He was crying, he had not had a shave or a wash and his breakfast tray was still on the table. He hadn't eaten anything. He seemed confused and was very uncomfortable. I find this situation totally unacceptable and I ask you to investigate his case thoroughly.

For a formal complaint, please complete the form and return it to	Signed: *Deidre Hynd*	Date: 22.5.10

---

2 Read the complaint in Section 3 and answer these questions.

    1 Which ADLs does the patient need help with?
    2 What is the daughter's complaint about?
    3 How does Nurse Jones feel about his job?
    4 What does Ms Hynd want the Patient Relations Department to do?
    5 What advice would you give to Nurse Jones?

Pronunciation **3** 🔘 **44** The Complaints Board criticised the nurse for not showing empathy towards his patient. Read this definition, then listen to three nurses talking to their patients. How much empathy do they demonstrate?

> **empathy** (*n*) The ability to imagine yourself in the position of another person and so to share and understand that person's feelings – (compare with *sympathy* and *understanding*).

Longman Dictionary of Contemporary English

	no empathy	a little empathy	a lot of empathy
Nurse 1			
Nurse 2			
Nurse 3			

4 Work in pairs and compare your answers. How do the nurses show empathy?

5 Listen again. What problems do the patients have? How do they feel? Complete the summaries with the words in the box.

depressing	embarrassed	feeding himself	humiliating
sickness	washing her hair		

1 Shaminder is having problems _____ with a knife and fork. He doesn't want people to see him eating with a spoon because he finds it

_____ .

2 Sheila is having problems _____ by herself. She feels a little

_____ .

3 Josh is suffering from _____ due to his chemotherapy. He finds it _____ .

Vocabulary

6 Reorder the words to make expressions that nurses use to improve communication with patients. Read audio script 44 on page 76 to check your answers.

Showing empathy
1 how you / feeling / I understand / must be
2 for you / it's difficult / I can see

Reassuring
3 clean you up / much better / Let me / don't worry Josh / and you'll feel / Please
4 be embarrassed, Sheila. / happen to anyone. / It can / Don't
5 of my job / I'm used / it's part / to it;

Respecting the patient's privacy
6 come back / Do you / later? / want me to
7 a screen / have / a little privacy. / to put round the bed. / I'll bring / You can

7 Look at the pairs of adjectives in the box. The adjective ending in *-ed* describes the patient's feeling and the adjective in in *-ing* describes the situation. Complete these sentences with an appropriate adjective in the box.

depressing / depressed	embarrassing / embarrassed
frustrating / frustrated	humiliating / humiliated

1 Shaminder thinks it is _____ when other people see him eat with a spoon.
2 He feels _____ that he can't eat normally.
3 Sheila feels _____ because she can't wash her hair by herself.
4 Josh feels _____ because of the chemotherapy.
5 It is _____ for patients when they find they can't do everyday things.
6 For many people, it can be _____ if they can't have some privacy to get dressed or even brush their teeth.

Wound management

1 Number the pictures 1–6 to show the correct order for cleaning a wound.

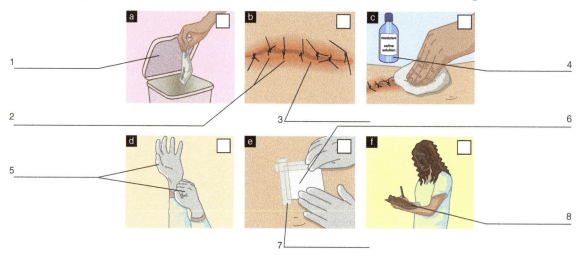

2 🔘 **45** Before you listen, read and complete the nurse's half of the dialogue with the words in the box. Then listen and check your answers. Label the pictures in 1 with the words in the box.

absorbent dressing	antibiotics	bin	disposable gloves
dressing	edges	pus	saline solution	sutures	tape
wound assessment chart	wound

Nurse: Great, thanks Ms Hagans. So how are things after your operation? Let's see, you've had your appendix removed – is that right?

Patient: Yes, the painkillers make me feel a bit nauseous, but I'm OK. Just the area around the wound is a little itchy.

Nurse: Yes it will be; it's a good sign – it means the [1]_____ is healing, so there's no infection and you don't need any [2]_____ .

Patient: That's good to know.

Nurse: Sorry, just give me a minute to put on my [3]_____ . Right. Let me see, you've got [4]_____ and we need to change your [5]_____ every day. Before I start, can I just ask you is the wound painful at all?

Patient: Like I said, it's a bit itchy, but it really doesn't hurt very much. I can hardly feel it at all.

Nurse: So on a scale of one to ten, how painful is it?

Patient: Two maybe.

Nurse: Two. OK. Now, I'm just going to remove the old dressing and then we can clean the wound. I'll just pop that in the [6]_____ . Erm, it all looks very clean and healthy … good. There's no [7]_____ or bad odour and the [8]_____ are joining up nicely.

Patient: Uh huh.

Nurse: I'm going to use some [9]_____ just to clean the wound. I'll try to do it gently. Let me know if you want me to stop. OK, Ms Hagans, I'm just going to clean that up and put the [10]_____ on. How's that for you?

Patient: Good, yes, thanks.

Nurse: I just need to secure the dressing with some [11]_____ . There we go. Let me just fill in your [12]_____ and we're done.

3 Work in pairs. Read Una Hagens's Wound Assessment and Treatment chart, using a dictionary to help you. Complete as much information as you can and then listen again to complete the chart.

Wound Assessment & Treatment Chart		28.07.2010			
Name	Ms Una Hagans		DOB: 25.09.1958		
Type of wound	traumatic	surgical	burn	diabetic ulcer	pressure ulcer	other
Location of wound:	abdomen					
Infection	yes	no				
Dressing frequency	twice a day	3 times a day	daily		every 3rd day	
Antibiotics	no	yes	oral	IV		
Odour	yes	slight	no			
Pain assessment	1 – 2 – 3 – 4 – 5 – 6 – 7 – 8 – 9 – 10					
Wound closure	sutures	clips	open wound			
Wound dressing	NAD	antimicrobial	hydrating	absorbent		
Comments	feels nauseous – painkillers					

Mia Fox, 19, student
Burn to the left arm, following an accident in the kitchen. The wound has become infected and inflamed, but there is no odour. The patient feels moderate pain – 3/10 on the pain scale.
Apply antimicrobial dressing – change in two days' time – oral antibiotics.

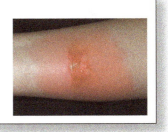

4 Read the case history and fill in the chart for Mia Fox.

Wound Assessment & Treatment Chart					
Name			DOB:		
Type of wound	traumatic	surgical	burn	diabetic ulcer	pressure ulcer	other
Location of wound:	left _____					
Infection	yes	no				
Dressing frequency	3 times a day	twice a day	once a day		every 3rd day	
Antibiotics	no	yes	oral	IV		
Odour	yes	slight	no			
Pain assessment	1 – 2 – 3 – 4 – 5 – 6 – 7 – 8 – 9 – 10					
Wound closure	sutures	clips	open wound			
Wound dressing	NAD	antimicrobial	hydrating	absorbent		
Comments						

5 Work in pairs. Use the prompts to assess the wound and apply the dressing for Mia Fox. Swap roles.

1 Introduce yourself – ask patient to confirm identity.
2 Ask the patient what happened. Ask the patient about pain.
3 Explain what you are going to do. Reassure the patient.
4 Change the dressing – explain what you are doing.

7 Elimination
• assess patient elimination
• describe bowel movements
• assess diarrhoea
• present a patient case

Assessing patient elimination

Reading **1** Look at the nursing assessment. What is Mrs Ashton suffering from? What do you think is the cause of the problem?

Birmingham General Hospital

Nursing assessment
Name: Eileen Ashton
Height: 162 cm   **Weight:** 65 kg

Mrs Eileen Ashton, 76 years, is a widow of six months living alone. Her children and grandchildren live 100 km away. She doesn't cook for herself, but enjoys cooking when her family visit. She often has a diet of just soup and toast. She has problems sleeping and gets little exercise, although previously was fairly active. She states she has a bowel movement about every three to four days and her stools are small, hard lumps and painful to pass. She is suffering from abdominal pain.

Vocabulary **2** People use different formal and informal expressions to talk about elimination. Complete the sentences with the words in the box. Use a dictionary to help you.

bathroom	bowel	constipation	defecate	diarrhoea	incontinent
poo	runs	urinate	urine	waterworks	wee

1 In the USA, we say 'go to the b_____', but British people say 'go to the toilet'.
2 'Mummy, can I go to the toilet? I need a w_____ !'.
3 U_____ is the medical word for wee or pee. The verb is to u_____ . We can also use the term 'to pass water'.
4 Mr Jones complains of trouble with his w_____ . He can't always control his bladder and is sometimes i_____ .
5 'Have you had a b_____ movement today, Mrs Davis?'
6 A stool or a motion is the medical word for a p_____ . The verb is to d_____ .
7 A patient with a loose stool has d_____ ; but a patient with very hard stools could have c_____ .
8 'I've got the r_____ , nurse. I have to go to the toilet all the time.'

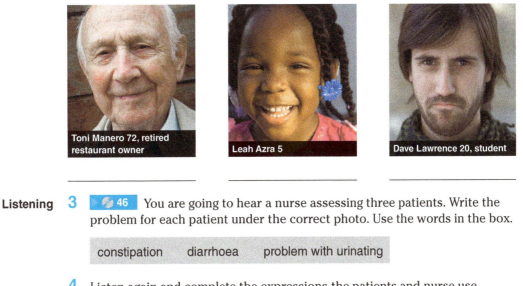

Toni Manero 72, retired restaurant owner

Leah Azra 5

Dave Lawrence 20, student

_____   _____   _____

Listening **3** 🔊 **46** You are going to hear a nurse assessing three patients. Write the problem for each patient under the correct photo. Use the words in the box.

> constipation   diarrhoea   problem with urinating

4 Listen again and complete the expressions the patients and nurse use.

1 Well, I've had problems _____ .
2 Leah, did you _____ this morning?
3 I did a _____ .
4 Well, basically, I've had _____ ever since I came back from holiday.

5 Rewrite the sentences 1–4 above using more formal / medical language. Use the language from 2 to help you.

Grammar **6** Write the past participle for each verb.

be	catch	come	do	eat	go	have	notice	open	pass
been	_____	_____	_____	_____	_____	_____	_____	_____	_____

7 Complete the nurse's questions using four of the past participles from 6.

1 How have you __*been*__ for the last few days?
2 Have you _____ water today?
3 Mrs Azra, have you _____ any blood … ?
4 Has she _____ in any pain?
5 How long have you _____ the diarrhoea exactly?
6 How many times have you _____ a bowel movement today?

8 Match the questions 1–6 in 7 with these answers a–f. Write the name of the patient. Then listen to the dialogues again and check your answers.

a) A little, yeah.   ☐3️⃣ _Leah_____

b) Yes, yes she has. It's a bit worrying.   ☐ _____

c) About four or five times.   ☐ _____

d) Yes, but only a few drops.   ☐ _____

e) Since Tuesday evening.   ☐ _____

f) I've had problems with my waterworks again. ☐ _____

Describing bodily functions

Vocabulary **1** Some patients, for example children, are more comfortable when nurses use familiar language. Rewrite sentences 1–6 using one of the familiar terms in the box. There is more than one possible answer.

go to the toilet / bathroom	poo	waterworks	wee

1 Is it painful for you to defecate?
2 Do you often have to get up to urinate in the night?
3 Have you noticed any blood in your urine?
4 How many times a day do you pass a motion?
5 She's been having problems with urination and bladder control.
6 Do you have hard stools?

Listening **2** 🔘 **47** Active listening is an important skill for nurses. Staff Nurse Paul is checking up on his patient, Ms Sonoda. Read this definition and complete the dialogue with the phrases in the box. Listen to check and then underline examples of active listening techniques in the dialogue.

> ### Active Listening is …
> … showing your patient that you are really listening to him or her. Use encouraging expressions such as 'I see' and 'go on' or sounds like 'uh-huh?' Use non verbal signals such as nodding your head or smiling warmly. Silence and repeating your patient's words are also useful techniques.

anything else	can you describe	Could you explain
I understand	take your time	

Staff Nurse: Is there [1]_____ , Ms Sonoda; you look a bit worried? (*smiles warmly*)

Ms Sonoda: Erm, (*long pause*) I'm sorry; it's very embarrassing for me to talk about.

Nurse: Don't worry, [2]_____.

Ms Sonoda: I have some pain.

Nurse: Pain?

Ms Sonoda: Yes, I have pains, just here when I go to the toilet and then it stops.

Nurse: [3]_____ what you mean?

Ms Sonoda: Well, I go to the toilet and it's very painful. But then afterwards the pain is gone.

Nurse: I see. (*short pause*) And [4]_____ your bowel movements?

Ms Sonoda: Erm, yes. No, I'm sorry …

Nurse: (*nods*) [5]_____ this isn't an easy thing to talk about. (*short pause*) A normal bowel movement is where there is no pain and the stools are soft and easy to pass.

Ms Sonoda: (*long pause*) No, no, its not like that.

Nurse: OK. (*short pause*) When you go to the toilet are the stools small and hard
or runny?

Ms Sonoda: Well, very runny.

Speaking **3** Practise the dialogue in pairs. Pay attention to your active listening techniques and remember to use patient-friendly intonation.

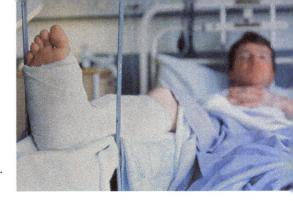

Listening **4** 🎧 **48** Christophe is recovering from a broken leg following a motorcycle accident. Listen to Part 1 of Staff Nurse Paula Willis' assessment and answer these questions.

1 Christophe usually has a / an _____ bowel movement.
2 Christophe is suffering from constipation because …
3 Christophe hasn't had a bowel movement …

Language

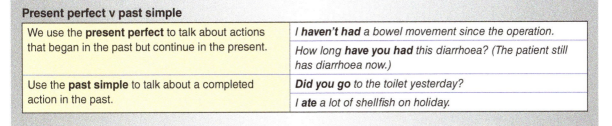

Present perfect v past simple	
We use the **present perfect** to talk about actions that began in the past but continue in the present.	*I **haven't had** a bowel movement since the operation.*
	*How long **have you had** this diarrhoea? (The patient still has diarrhoea now.)*
Use the **past simple** to talk about a completed action in the past.	***Did you go** to the toilet yesterday?*
	*I **ate** a lot of shellfish on holiday.*

5 Complete the nurse's assessment questions. Listen again to check.

1 How long _____ you _____ like this?
2 _____ you _____ your bowels today?
3 When _____ you last _____ your bowels?
4 How long _____ you _____ in hospital now?

6 You are Christophe. Write answers to the questions in 5. Begin you answers with *I* … and write full sentences.

7 🎧 **49** Listen to Part 2 of the assessment. Then read the statements below and underline the correct verb form (past simple or present perfect).

1 Christophe *has been / was* in hospital since 5th May.
2 He *didn't go / hasn't been* to the toilet for a few days.
3 He *felt / has felt* bloated for two days.
4 And he last *had / has had* a bowel movement a week ago.
5 Christophe *hasn't eaten / didn't eat* anything last night.
6 In fact, the patient *hasn't eaten / didn't eat* anything since yesterday lunchtime.

Writing **8** Read Paula's patient summary. Correct the five mistakes in the text.

> *juice*
> Christophe has not eaten anything since three days and has only drunk ~~coffee~~ for breakfast. His stools have been small and soft and he needs to push to defecate. He has experienced pain going to the toilet and he suffered abdominal pain this morning.

9 Write the whole assessment, including the correct information from 8. Answer these questions.

1 Why is Christophe in hospital?
2 How long has he been in hospital?
3 How has he felt for the last two days?
4 What has he eaten and drunk / not eaten and drunk for the last three days?
5 Describe his stools and any other symptoms.

Diarrhoea

Speaking **1** Write a definition of diarrhoea. Do you think it is a dangerous condition? How can you treat it? Compare your ideas with a partner.

Reading **2** Read this article. Complete the sentences with a word from the article.

1 Diarrhoeal disease is the r_____ of an intestinal infection.
2 After pneumonia, diarrhoea is the second main c_____ of death in children under five in developing countries.
3 Diarrhoea c_____ a patient to become dehydrated.
4 If body fluids and electrolytes aren't replaced, severe dehydration can r_____ in death.

Diarrhoea

The definition of diarrhoea is when a person passes three or more loose or liquid stools per day. It is a common condition which most people suffer from at some time in their lives. Diarrhoea is a result of an infection in the intestine, which can be caused by bacteria, a virus, or some kind of parasite. In developed countries, an episode of diarrhoea is usually not very difficult to control and is not usually considered dangerous. In developing countries, however, diarrhoeal disease is one of the main causes of child mortality. In children under five years old, diarrhoeal disease is the second main cause of death – second only to pneumonia.

Because most cases of diarrhoea are caused by viruses, it's not usually possible to use antibiotics to treat them. Diarrhoea caused by bacteria will usually go away in a few days even without antibiotics. In fact, the most dangerous thing about diarrhoea is that it causes a patient to become dehydrated. A person suffering from diarrhoea quickly loses lots of water and electrolytes (sodium, chloride, potassium and bicarbonate) – the essential chemicals that allow the body to work. If the lost fluid and electrolytes are not replaced, the patient becomes dehydrated.

There are three stages of dehydration:

1 Early dehydration
- the patient is thirsty and may have a headache

2 Moderate dehydration
- the patient is very thirsty
- the patient is restless or irritable
- the patient's skin becomes less elastic
- the patient's eyes are sunken

3 Severe dehydration
- the patients' symptoms become more severe
- The patient goes into shock, the skin is pale and damp, the pulse is rapid and weak, blood pressure is very low

Severe dehydration can result in death if body fluids and electrolytes are not replaced. In developing countries, children who die from diarrhoea often also suffer from malnutrition, which makes them weak so it is easier for them to get diarrhoea. However, each time they get diarrhoea, it makes their malnutrition even worse. It is not surprising, therefore, that diarrhoea is one of the main causes of malnutrition in children under five years old.

Vocabulary **3** Complete this word-building table with words from the article in 2. Then use words from the table to complete sentences 1–5.

Noun	Verb	Adjective
diarrhoea		1_____
2_____	to dehydrate	dehydrated
3_____		intestinal
replacement	4_____	
loss	5_____	lost

1 A severe attack of diarrhoea can result in _____ .
2 The _____ of fluid and electrolytes can cause the body to become dehydrated.
3 Diarrohea is caused by an infection of the _____ .
4 The _____ of the body fluids lost during and attack of diarrhoea is essential to the patient's recovery.
5 _____ disease is one of the main causes of child mortality in developing countries.

Listening **4** 🎧 **50** Listen to Femi Lwanga talking about her experiences of treating diarrhoea in children.

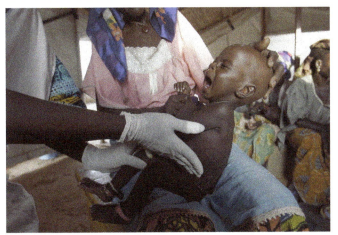

ORS = oral rehydration salts

1 Where does she work and what is the biggest problem there?
2 What condition does she treat with ORS?

Vocabulary **5** Complete Femi's explanation about the treatment of diarrhoea with the words in the box. Listen again to check your answers.

| cheap   dehydration   drip   faeces   fluids   rehydrate   replaces   sugar |

The most important thing in treating diarrhoea is to ¹_____ the patient. A severely dehydrated patient needs rehydration with intravenous ²_____ . They go into the hospital here and have an intravenous ³_____ . For moderate dehydration, it is possible to treat a patient effectively with oral rehydration salts or ORS. We have saved a lot of lives, particularly children's lives with this. ORS is a mixture of clean water, salt and ⁴_____, which is very easy to prepare even here where we have such limited medical facilities. It is very ⁵_____ , which is also important. As I often have to explain, ORS does not stop the diarrhoea, but it stops the dangerous ⁶_____ caused by the diarrhoea. It is absorbed in the small intestine and ⁷_____ the water and electrolytes lost in the ⁸_____ .

Presenting a patient case

Language **1** Charge Nurse David Amani presents a patient case to his colleagues. Complete Part 1 of his presentation with the correct form (past simple or present perfect) of the verbs in brackets.

> Next, in cubicle four, we have Mrs Eileen Ashton. She prefers 'Eileen'. She's seventy-six and ¹_____ (*present*) at 14.45 with abdominal pain. Eileen ²_____ (*become*) a widow six months ago and now lives alone. Since the death of her husband, Eileen ³_____ (*not cook*) for herself and ⁴_____ (*be*) on a diet of soup and toast. She ⁵_____ (*be*) relatively active in the past, but ⁶_____ (*not take*) regular exercise for several months. In addition, she ⁷_____ (*suffer*) from insomnia for the last six months.

Writing **2** Use these prompts to write Part 2 of David's presentation. Make sure you use the correct form of the verbs.

1 on admission / Eileen / complain / abdominal pain
2 Dr Insulza saw her at 16.00 / she / rate / pain seven out of ten / on pain scale
3 her last bowel movement / be / four days ago
4 she / open / her bowels / every three or four days / since / beginning of May
5 she / describe / her stools / as hard lumps / Type one on the Bristol Stool Chart
6 Eileen / experience / some pain / no blood or mucus

Listening **3** 🔊 **51** Triage Nurse, Magda Nowak, is assessing her patient, Anita Blasky. Listen to Part 1 and circle the correct answer.

1 What are the patient's symptoms?
stomach ache / frequent bowel movement / headache
2 How does the patient feel about her problem?
embarrassed / angry / sad
3 What is your nursing diagnosis of the patient?
constipation / diarrhoea

Speaking **4** Read the beginning of the nursing assessment. Write five assessment questions that Magda asked to obtain this information. Work in pairs. Practise asking and answering your questions.

Example: *How long have you suffered from …?*

Nursing assessment   b **Birmingham** **General Hospital**

Anita Blasky is seventeen years old and studying for her university entrance exam. She is suffering from frequent bowel movements and visits the toilet ten to twelve times a day (five times this morning). Anita also wakes up several times a night to defecate. Her symptoms began four months ago and are intermittent. The stools are very loose, almost liquid, Type 6 on the Bristol Stool Chart. The patient also experiences some cramping.

Listening **5** 🎧 **52** Listen to Part 2 of the interview and complete the second part of the nursing assessment with the words in the box.

| allergies | angry | embarrassed | kilos | laxatives | overweight |
| spicy | weight |

Anita does not suffer from food [1]_____ *and rarely eats* [2]_____ *foods. She is trying to lose* [3]_____ *and so far has lost five* [4]_____ *. She feels she is* [5]_____ *and seems to have a negative body image. She appears* [6]_____ *when asked about her body weight. She is continuing to diet and often uses* [7]_____ *. Anita finds it difficult to discuss her symptoms and is noticeably* [8]_____ *about her use of laxatives.*

Speaking **6** What is your nursing diagnosis of Anita Blasky's condition? What treatment can you suggest? Work in pairs and discuss.

7 Compare your ideas with the rest of the group.

8 Choose one of the patients from page 53 (Toni, Leah or Dave) and prepare a presentation of the patient case.

1 Practise giving the presentation together. Use staging words from Unit 4.
2 When you are ready, present your patient case to the class. Include this information.

- patient name / age / DOB
- pain scale
- patient stools
- patient symptoms
- when patient came for treatment
- diagnosis

Patient discharge

- evaluate levels of independence
- talk about a patient discharge plan
- explain medication
- make appointments on the phone

Evaluating levels of independence

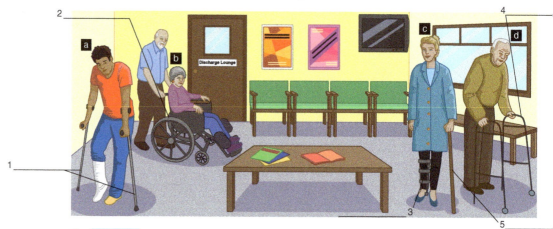

Listening   **1**   🔘 **53**   Look at the picture of patients in the discharge lounge and listen. Label the patients a–d with their names.

Elin	Jim	Mr Aziz	Mrs Ridley

2   Listen again. Who …

1 fell off a ladder?
2 has painful knees?
3 can't remember much about the accident?
4 has had a hip operation?
5 has had lots of physiotherapy?
6 is rather frail?

Vocabulary   **3**   Label the mobility aids 1–5 used by the patients in the picture with the words in the box.

crutches	leg brace	walking frame	walking stick	wheelchair

4   Look at the pictures of mobility aids for the home. Label them with the words in the box.

bath lift	grab bar	non-slip mat	raised toilet seat	shower chair

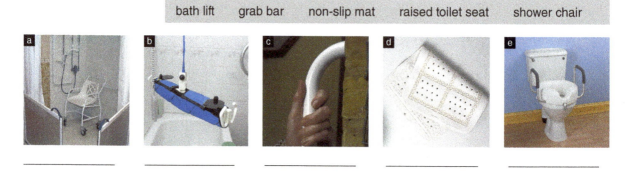

_____   _____   _____   _____   _____

5 Match the descriptions a–e to the mobility aids for the home in 4.

    a) It stops the patient slipping in the bath or shower.
    b) It lets the patient slide onto the toilet from a chair.
    c) It lowers the patient into the bath.
    d) It allows the patient to take a shower sitting down.
    e) It gives the patient something to hold on to / pull themselves up by / steady themselves with.

Listening   **6**   🔊 54   Nurse, Denis Astorga is preparing three of his patients for discharge. Listen to the three dialogues. Which of the patients from 1 is he talking to / about?

1 _____   2 _____   3 _____

7 Listen again. What are the patients / carers worried about – bathing, toileting or dressing? Circle the correct answers. Write the mobility aid(s) the nurse recommends.

1	bathing	toileting	dressing	_____
2	bathing	toileting	dressing	_____
3	bathing	toileting	dressing	_____

8 Match the beginnings of the sentences from the dialogue 1–6 with the correct endings a–f.

1 How do you feel about washing …   a) going to the toilet.
2 It's going to be difficult for me to…   b) we discharge you.
3 Why don't you try taking …   c) lift her on and off the toilet.
4 It's a good idea to …   d) your shower sitting down?
5 She's going to need help with …   e) install grab bars around the bath.
6 You need to practise before …   f) and dressing?

9 Listen and check. Which expressions …

1 are suggestions and recommendations made by the nurse? *(four expressions)*
2 are questions the nurse asks the patient? *(one expression)*
3 are worries and concerns expressed by the patient or carer? *(one expression)*

Speaking   **10** Work in pairs. Take turns to be the patient / carer and the nurse and to give advice about mobility aids in the situations below. Use the language from 5–7 to help you. Begin like this:

Nurse: So, do you think you're going to manage at home? Is there anything you are worried about?
Patient: Well nurse …

1 My wife has problems getting in and out of the bath.
2 I don't need a wheelchair anymore, but my legs are still very stiff.
3 We've only got a shower at home, but I'm too weak to stand for very long.
4 I'm very independent, but I'm nervous about taking a bath by myself. I'm worried I could slip.
5 My husband is heavy. How can I help him get to the toilet from his wheelchair?
6 We can do everything else, but I just don't know how we're going to get him into the bath.

A patient discharge plan

Speaking **1** What usually happens before and after a patient is discharged in your country? Work in pairs and discuss.

Reading **2** Read the patient information about patient discharge. Match the missing titles a–e to the paragraphs in the leaflet.

a) Special equipment
b) Family support
c) Problems to watch out for
d) Follow-up appointments
e) Taking medication

---

med*TRUST* hospital

Your Discharge Plan

1 Post-discharge care
After you are discharged you may be living at home or in another setting. It is important to know where to find care and also to know who will help you after your discharge from hospital.

2 _____
It is important to understand your prescription drugs – when to take them and what side effects you might experience. Ask for the name and number of the person to call in case you have any questions. Tell the hospital staff about the medication you took before coming to hospital. This includes over-the-counter drugs and prescription drugs as well as any supplements. Ask if you can still take them after your discharge.

3 _____
It is important to know what medical equipment, e.g. walking stick, you will need to use after your discharge. You may have some questions about this after you leave hospital, so ask for the name and number of the person to call.

4 _____
What if you have problems after your discharge? Do you know what they might be and how to deal with them? Ask for the name and number of the person to call if you experience problems.

5 Helping with special tasks
How do you feel about using medical equipment, giving a shot or changing a bandage? If you are unsure, ask a nurse to show you. Then, demonstrate to the nurse that you can also do it. Ask for the name and number of the person to call if you need help after your discharge from hospital.

6 _____
Maybe you are worried about how you and your family are going to deal with your illness. Ask your nurse about support groups in your area. If necessary, ask to talk to a therapist before you leave hospital.

7 Contacting your healthcare provider
Write down the name and telephone number of the doctor or healthcare provider you should contact if you have problems or questions.

8 _____
It is important to find out which tests and / or appointments you need in the weeks that follow your discharge from hospital.

---

3 Match the definitions below with one of the highlighted words in the text.

1 medication you can buy without a prescription _____
2 medication your doctor gives you _____
3 vitamins or iron tablets, for example _____
4 problems caused by medication _____
5 to inject medication or drugs _____
6 a group of people who have the same problems and provide help to each other _____
7 a person who helps people feel better / grow stronger, particularly after an illness _____
8 doctor or nurse, for example _____

Listening **4** [🎧 55] Listen to a nurse going through Nancy Lorenz's discharge plan with her. Are these statements *true* (T) or *false* (F)? Correct the false statements.

1 The patient isn't worried about going home. (T / F)
2 The patient lives with her sister. (T / F)
3 The patient's sister will help her with her ADLs. (T / F)
4 The patient's neighbour will help her with the cooking. (T / F)

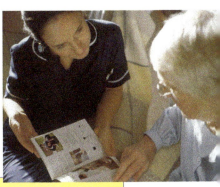

Independence assessment			
Bathing	Independent ☐	Needs assistance ☐	Dependent ☐
Ambulation*	Independent ☐	Needs assistance ☐	Dependent ☐
Toileting	Independent ☐	Needs assistance ☐	Dependent ☐
Transferring**	Independent ☐	Needs assistance ☐	Dependent ☐
Eating	Independent ☐	Needs assistance ☐	Dependent ☐
Dressing	Independent ☐	Needs assistance ☐	Dependent ☐

* getting around on foot
** getting around by vehicle

5 Listen again and complete the assessment form in 4. Tick (✓) the correct boxes.

Language

Zero conditional

Use the **zero conditional** (*if* + present tense + present tense) to offer solutions to a problem or to give instructions.	*Who **can I call** if I **have** a problem?*
	*If you **have** any questions, **call** the helpline.*

First conditional

Use the **first conditional** (*if* + present tense + *will*) to describe a situation and its possible result.	*My husband **will help me** if I have problems.*
	*If I get tired, **I'll have** a rest.*

6 Try to remember how Nancy described her worries and complete these first conditional sentences.

1 If I have problems, my sister …
2 If I'm not careful in the shower, …
3 I won't have the energy for cooking if …
4 If I need help with the shopping, my neighbour …

7 Make zero conditional sentences with 1–5 to offer Nancy advice or give instructions.

1 If you're worried about slipping in the shower, …
2 If you have any questions, …
3 Eat fruit and drink water if …
4 Make sure you rest if …
5 If you need to go shopping, …

8 Check your answers to 6 and 7 by looking at audio script 55 on pages 78–79.

Explaining medication

Listening **1** 🔊 **56** Nancy Lorenz is going to be discharged from hospital this morning. A nurse is talking to her about her medication and post-discharge care. Listen and circle the best answers.

1 How does Nancy feel today?
   a) worried b) better c) ill
2 The capsules that the doctor is going to give Nancy are
   a) antibiotics b) painkillers c) laxatives
3 The tablets are for
   a) constipation b) pain c) infection
4 The laxative syrup is for
   a) pain b) constipation c) infection
5 Who will get Nancy's medication for her?
   a) her brother-in-law b) her sister c) her neighbour
6 Why does Nancy need to visit the Outpatient Clinic?
   a) to see her specialist b) to have her stitches taken out
   c) to check on her diet

Vocabulary **2** Label the different types of medication. Use the words in the box.

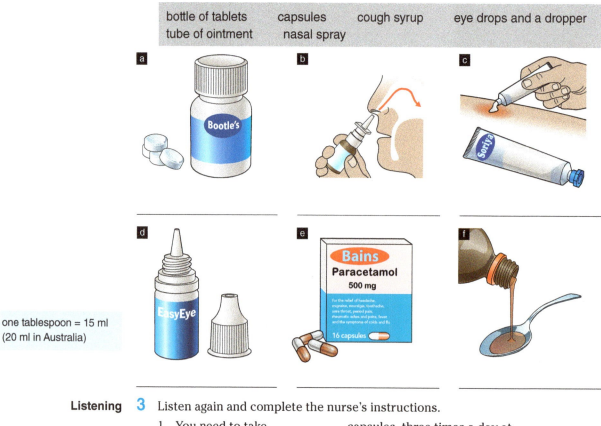

| bottle of tablets | capsules | cough syrup | eye drops and a dropper |
| tube of ointment | nasal spray | | |

a

b

c

Bootle's

Sortya

d

e

f

EasyEye

Bains
Paracetamol
500 mg

for the relief of headache,
migraine, neuralgia, toothache,
sore throat, period pain,
rheumatic aches and pains, fever
and the symptoms of colds and flu

16 capsules

one tablespoon = 15 ml
(20 ml in Australia)

_____   _____   _____

Listening **3** Listen again and complete the nurse's instructions.

1 You need to take _____ capsules, three times a day at _____ .
2 If you're in _____ then take _____ tablets.
3 Don't take more than two every six _____ , and no more than eight tablets a _____ .
4 You need to _____ this on twice a day – in the morning when you get up and at night when you go to bed.
5 Apply it to the area where your _____ are.
6 You need to take a _____ three times a day at mealtimes.

1

KOLD KARMA
Cold and flu capsules

Directions

How to take:
For oral use.
Swallow capsules with water.
Do not chew.

How much to take:
Adults and children over 12:
Two capsules to be taken every
four hours. Do not exceed
eight capsules in 24 hours.

Children 6–12 years: One
capsule every four hours.
Do not exceed four capsules
in 24 hours. Do not give to
children under six years.

2

DICALM
Diarrhoea tablets

Directions

The tablets should be chewed
followed by a glass of water.

Adults, the elderly and children
12 years and over: two tablets.
Children 6–12 years: one tablet.
Not to be given to children
under six years.

To be taken every two to four
hours as required according to
the severity of the symptoms.

Do not exceed six doses in
24 hours.

3

COFFALIX
Cough syrup

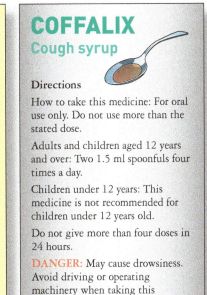

Directions

How to take this medicine: For oral
use only. Do not use more than the
stated dose.

Adults and children aged 12 years
and over: Two 1.5 ml spoonfuls four
times a day.

Children under 12 years: This
medicine is not recommended for
children under 12 years old.

Do not give more than four doses in
24 hours.

DANGER: May cause drowsiness.
Avoid driving or operating
machinery when taking this
medicine.

Reading **4** Read the directions for three over-the-counter medications. Find phrases that
mean the following.

1 Don't take this medicine more than four times in twenty-four hours.
2 It can make you feel sleepy. Don't drive when you are taking this medicine.
3 Swallow whole.
4 Take this medicine when you need it according to how bad you feel.
5 Only take this medicine by mouth.

Writing **5** Write simple instructions for the appropriate medication for the people below.
Use imperatives – *take, don't take, you need to,* etc.

1 a 44-year-old man with bad diarrhoea
2 the father of an eight-year-old girl with a cold
3 a 50-year-old taxi driver with flu symptoms and a bad cough
4 a 30-year-old woman with a cold
5 an 11-year-old with diarrhoea

Speaking **6** Match these questions and answers.

1 What medication is Keiko taking?
2 How often does she need her medication?
3 What's the dosage?

a) every four hours
b) two 80 mg tablets
c) Oxycontin, for pain relief

7 Work in pairs. Take turns to practise asking and answering questions like those
in 6. Use the directions for over-the-counter medications in 4.

Making appointments on the phone

Speaking **1** Orthopaedic Nurse Zafar Hussein is discharging his patient. He needs to make a phone call to book an appointment for him. Look at the information below (1–4) and brainstorm expressions for each item in the checklist.

1 His patient needs to see the practice nurse at his local Health Centre.
2 The appointment should be in about ten days' time.
3 The date today is 14 January.
4 The patient's name is Mr Ernesto Chavaz and he would prefer a morning appointment.

Making an Appointment Checklist

1 Greet person
2 Identify yourself and department/unit   *This is Zafar from Orthopaedics.*
3 Give reason for calling
4 Suggest day and time
5 Confirm day and time
6 Give patient details
7 Thank person and end call

Listening **2** 🔊 **57** Listen to the call and compare your answers in 1.

3 🔊 **58** You are now going to hear Zafar making another appointment for a different patient. Listen and tick (✓) the points you hear.

Making an Appointment Checklist

☐ Greet person
☐ Identify self and department/unit
☐ Give reason for calling
☐ Suggest day and time
☐ Confirm day and time
☐ Give patient details
☐ Thank person and end call

4 Complete the patient's appointment card. Then complete the statements 1–3 by underlining the correct expression in italics.

1 Sandra is the receptionist in the *Occupational Therapy / Physiotherapy Unit.*
2 The therapist only works on *Tuesdays and Thursdays / Tuesdays and Wednesdays.*
3 The nurse suggests an appointment after *5.00 in the afternoon / 3.30 in the afternoon.*

Your Next Appointment

Patient Name: _____
Appointment with: _____
Day: _____
Date: _____
Time: _____

5 🔊 59 You are going to hear Zafar changing Mr Pattern's appointment. Write the expression the speakers use to …

1 ask to change the time of the appointment.
2 check the appointment details.
3 ask the caller to wait.

Pronunciation **6** In English, we stress the words (or syllables in a word) we want to emphasise. Listen again and underline the stressed words (or syllables) in these sentences.

1 Sorry, did you say Tuesday or Thursday?
2 Tuesday, Tuesday afternoon.
3 No, not ten fifteen, ten fifty.
4 Oh, OK, ten fifty, sorry.

7 Listen again. Check and repeat the sentences with the correct stress pattern.

Speaking **8** Work in small groups. Discuss these questions.

1 How do you feel about speaking on the phone in English?
A: *I find it difficult because* …
2 What advice would you give to someone when speaking on the phone?
A: *Smile* …

9 Work in pairs. Student A, look at the information below. Student B, turn to page 69.

Student A

1 Your patient, Islam Raba, has had a lung operation. You are discharging him, but he will need a new dressing next week. Phone his local doctor's surgery and make an appointment with the practice nurse to change his dressing in five days' time. Mr Raba prefers an appointment between 14.45 and 16.00 on Wednesday 23 November because he has a physiotherapy appointment at the same surgery at 14.00. Use the checklist from page 66 to help you make the call.

2 Islam Raba can't come to the appointment you have made for him. Call the surgery again and reschedule his appointment for another day and time. He is free on Thursday 24 and Friday 25 November, but only in the afternoon – from 14.00 onwards. He needs a clean dressing by the end of the week.

3 You are the receptionist at the physiotherapy unit. Answer a call from Student B about an appointment with the consultant physiotherapist, Alex Green. Alex Green is very busy all week, but has free appointments on Wednesday 4 March at 10.30, Thursday 5 March at 16.30 and 17.30 and Friday 6 March at 9.30 and 11.45.

4 Answer a second call from Student B about changing the appointment. Alex Green is away on holiday from 9–19 March. There are appointments available with his colleague, Jana Martek, who is taking his place while he is away. She has appointments in the afternoon from 14.00 to 16.00. It isn't a problem for patients to bring small children to their appointments.

2 Pain

Pain assessment

Speaking exercise 6 page 15

Student B

1 Student A is your patient. Interview them about about their pain. Complete the pain map and pain scale on page 15. When you have finished, swap roles. You are the patient below and Student A will interview you about your pain.

2 You are Marie / Martin McKoewen and you are suffering from stomach pains. You feel a strong burning sensation that started an hour ago. The pain does not move and it is now much worse (7/10 on the pain scale). You often suffer from this type of pain, usually after you eat spicy food.

4 Symptoms

SOAP Notes

Speaking exercise 6 page 35

Student B

Dictate these nursing terms to Student A who will write the abbreviation.

1 right
2 blood sugar
3 three times a day
4 as required
5 left
6 range of motion
7 no known drug allergies
8 posterior / anterior

5 Food and nutrition

Offering advice on diet

Speaking exercise 8 page 43

Student B

1 You are Student A's doctor. Find out about their diet. Ask questions and make notes. Offer advice on how they can improve their diet.

2 You are Tony Rizzo and Student A is your doctor. Talk about your diet and answer the doctor's questions. Listen to their advice on how you can improve your diet.

Case history: Tony Rizzo, 54, is married with two teenage step-children and a newborn baby. He drives a taxi and as a result gets very little exercise. Tony complains of bad indigestion so his doctor has asked you to give him advice on a diet plan.

Food Journal: Tony Rizzo **BMI:** 25.5		
Tuesday	**Time**	**Typical Food Intake**
Breakfast	7.00	cereal, milky coffee, two slices white toast, boiled egg
Mid morning	10.30	tea, 3–4 chocolate biscuits
Lunch	12.30	burgers, chips, bread roll, carbonated drink, chocolate bar
Mid afternoon	15.00	tea, packet crisps
Dinner	19.00	steak, chips, fried tomatoes, piece of cake, cream
Evening	20.00+	3–5 coffees

6 Personal care

Activities of daily living

Speaking exercise 6 page 47

Student B

Begin by taking the role of the patient. Use the notes in checklist 2 to reply to Student A's questions. When you have finished, exchange roles. Ask Student A questions to complete the ADLs in checklist 1.

1

ADL Checklist			
Patient Name: Sophie Mellors		**Ward:** 1	
Function	**Independent**	**Needs Help**	**Dependent**
Bathing / Showering			
Dressing			
Grooming			
Oral Hygiene			
Toileting			

2

ADL Checklist			
Patient Name: Miles Denis		**Ward:** 2	
Function	**Independent**	**Needs Help**	**Dependent**
Bathing / Showering			*Bed bath*
Dressing			*Nurse to dress patient*
Grooming		*at bedside, help shaving*	
Oral Hygiene		*at bedside*	
Toileting		*Uses commode + urinal bottle*	

8 Patient discharge

Making appointments by telephone

Speaking exercise 9 page 67

Student B

1   You are the receptionist at the local doctor's surgery. Answer a call from Student A about an appointment with the practice nurse. The nurse has no free appointments between 14.00 and 16.00 on Wednesday 23 November, but she has appointments at 13.30 and 16.30.

2   Answer a second call from Student A about changing the appointment. The practice nurse is very busy on Thursday and Friday and has no appointments in the afternoons. She will take appointments after 18.00 on Thursday if a patient needs something urgently. She has appointments available at 15.30 and 17.00 on Monday 28 November.

3   You are the charge nurse in an orthopaedic ward. Your patient, Noor Ganem, has neck problems after a car accident. Phone the physiotherapy unit to make an appointment for an assessment with the consultant physiotherapist, Alex Green. Mrs Ganem is available between 10.00 and 12.00 on weekdays, except for Wednesday. Today is Tuesday 3 March. Use the checklist from page 66 to help you make the call.

4   Mrs Ganem forgot that it is the school holidays, so she is not available to come for an appointment before Monday 9 March. Call the physiotherapy unit to reschedule her appointment. She is only available when her children are at nursery, between 10.00 and 12.00 (except on Wednesdays).

Audio script

Unit 1 Patient admissions

⏺ 02

I work as an agency nurse and I specialise in renal care. This month I'm working in a transplant unit in Auckland, New Zealand, where I'm responsible for paediatric patients. I'm looking after a little girl at the moment who is waiting for a kidney transplant. I spend a lot of time with her; talking to her and explaining her condition. I carry out her tests and administer her medication every day, but we also play games … this week I'm teaching her to play dominoes. What do I like about my job? Well, I don't like dealing with the paperwork and there is a lot of it. Dealing with children can sometimes be very stressful, but it can also be very rewarding, too. I want to stay in renal care and I hope to qualify as an advanced practice nurse. In my free time, I go climbing, so you can usually find me in the mountains.

⏺ 03

physiotherapy	surgery	casualty
renal	neurology	geriatrics
radiology	pathology	paediatrics
cardiology	maternity	dermatology

⏺ 04

[V = Visitor; N = Nurse]

1 V: Excuse me; I'm looking for the canteen. Can you help me?
N: Yes, of course. Go straight on and it's in front of you, at the end of the corridor.

2 V: Excuse me, do you know where the Maternity Unit is?
N: It's on the second floor. Turn left here, go straight on, and when you get to the information desk, turn right. At the end of the corridor, turn right again and take Elevator A. The Maternity Unit is the first door on the left.

3 V: Hello. Do you know if there's a shop in the building? We want to buy some magazines.
N: Sure. Just turn left here and go down the corridor – there's a gift shop next to the pharmacy. You can buy magazines there, I think.

⏺ 05

From the 4th floor, the quickest way out is to take Elevator D down to the ground floor. Turn left out of the elevator, then right. At the information desk, turn left. Walk past the gift shop and the pharmacy on your left, and the entrance is opposite the main registration desk on your right.

⏺ 06

[P = Paramedic; N = Nurse]

1 P: This is Gupta. He fell off his motorbike. He's got problems with his left leg as you can see, but apart from that he's OK. He's just a just a bit shocked I think.
N: Hello Gupta. I need to fill in this form. Could you …

[M = Mother; P = Patient; N = Nurse]

2 M: I don't know how she did it. She was playing in the garden and she hit her head somehow. Her head is bleeding a lot.
P: My head hurts Mummy.
N: That doesn't look too bad, Kelly. But I need to clean your head so I can have a really good look at where it hurts. Could you …

[N = Nurse; P = Patient]

3 N: So, how many weeks pregnant are you Rosanna?
P: 23 weeks.
N: And what brings you here today?
P: I'm really worried. I'm bleeding and it hurts a lot. It's not normal. I'm worried about the baby.
N: The doctor will be with you in a few minutes. Could you …

[N = Nurse; P = Patient]

4 N: Can you tell me what happened, Mr Bradshaw?
P: I don't know. You know, I'm talking with this guy and then the next thing he hits me in the face. My eye really hurts.

⏺ 07

B, C, D, E, G, P, T, V, Z   F, L, M, N, S, X, Z   A, H, J, K
Q, U, W   I, Y   O   R

⏺ 08

[N = Nurse; P = Patient]

N: I'd like to check your personal details, if that's OK.
P: Of course.
N: Can you give me your full name please?
P: Rosanna Cameron.
N: Can you spell that please?
P: R-O-S-A double N-A, Cameron, C-A-M-E-R-O-N.
N: Can I just check, C-A-M for Max?
P: Yes.
N: E-R-O-N for Nigel?
P: Right.
N: And what would you like us to call you?
P: Rosanna is fine.
N: Rosanna, that sounds Italian. Where are you from?
P: I'm originally from Catagne in Sicily, but I came here for my studies, got married and now we're looking forward to our first child. I've been here for ten years already.
N: That's lovely. And what is your date of birth Rosanna?
P: The 20th of the first, 81.
N: Is that the 20th of January 1981?
P: That's right.
N: And what is your job?
P: International marketing manager for AXXA.
N: International marketing manager. OK. Now, I also need to ask, what's your marital status and who is your next of kin, to contact in an emergency?
P: I'm married and my husband, Daniel Cameron, is my next of kin. His mobile number is 0779 706 7517
N: Thank you. Do you have any allergies?
P: No.

09

[N = Nurse; R = Rosanna]

N: Here's your room, Rosanna. How are you feeling now?

R: Not so bad, just a bit tired.

N: Do you want to sit down and I'll show you where to put your things.

R: I've got a bag and two or three books.

N: Well, you can put your books on the shelf and your bag in the locker next to your bed. The buzzer is next to the light if you need my help.

R: Sorry, where's that? I don't see it.

N: Just here, above the chair.

R: OK. Is there a TV?

N: Yes, it's just here, next to the window.

R: Ah great, my husband can watch the tennis final when he comes to see me.

N: Well, for the TV you do need to buy a card from the gift shop.

R: Where's that, then?

N: On the ground floor, between the pharmacy and the waiting area.

R: Oh, OK.

N: Do you have any valuables?

R: No, no, just my watch. Oh, I have a mobile phone. Can I keep it with me?

N: Yes. You can put it in the drawer, just here above the locker, but you need to keep it switched off. The public phone is down the hall, on the left after the lift.

Unit 2 Pain

10

[N = Nurse; J = James]

1 N: So, where do you feel the pain, James?

J: My stomach, my chest. It's a really sharp pain that comes suddenly and is very strong.

N: OK … Can you point to where it hurts?

J: Yeah, it's here.

N: I see, so just there between your chest and your stomach. It sounds like indigestion, but let's …

[N = Nurse; G = Godfrey]

2 N: So, Godfrey. Can you tell me how you're feeling?

G: I'm still getting these headaches and they're getting worse and worse.

N: And where does it hurt?

G: Here at the front.

N: Where exactly?

G: On the right side, just above my eye.

[A = Alma; N = Nurse]

3 A: Nurse Kennedy?

N: Yes?

A: I'm in real pain, I'm sorry.

N: Where do you feel the pain, the same place?

A: Yeah, the back of my hip, the left one and then it shoots down my leg. It's really painful.

11

[M = Mr Turner]

1 T: I still have a headache. It's like a drum, a real throbbing pain.

[A = Abdul]

2 A: There's a dull ache in my lower back. It's quite a mild pain, but sometimes I can feel a shooting pain, like an electric shock.

[S = Shazia]

3 S: I get this burning feeling two or three hours after food and sometimes it's very sore. Sometimes it's very uncomfortable – quite a moderate pain – but other times it's only a bit more than uncomfortable.

[N = Nurse; C = Mrs Chen]

4 N: So the pain in your hands, Mrs Chen, what does it feel like?

C: It's a kind of tingling feeling, like pins and needles. I get it in my feet as well, but it's better than last week.

[N = Nurse; K = Karin]

5 N: Karin, tell me, are you in pain at the moment?

K: Yes, I am. It's here in my chest.

N: Can you describe it?

K: Yes, it's a stabbing pain, like a knife. It's a severe pain. It really hurts a lot.

12

[N = Nurse; D = Dina]

Part 1

N: Hello Dina. Come in and have a seat. And how's the little one today?

D: Ah, she's teething, so she screams a lot, I'm afraid.

N: Don't worry, it won't take long. I just want to ask you a few questions. Is that OK?

D: Yes of course. She's sleeping now anyway.

N: So, where does it hurt?

D: In my lower back. It's really painful sometimes.

N: Where exactly?

D: Here, just below my waist, it goes right across my back, like that.

N: Right. And can you describe the pain?

D: Yes, there's a dull ache and sometimes I feel a shooting pain, like an electric shock.

N: When did it start?

D: On Thursday.

N: Thursday and today it's, err ….. Monday, OK. Tell me, when do you feel the pain most?

D: Erm, I don't know.

N: All the time, at night, in the morning?

D: Often in the evenings.

N: I see. How long does it last, this pain?

D: One or two hours.

N: One or two hours, right.

13

[N = Nurse; D = Dina]

Part 2

D: I'm sorry. It's difficult 'cos I need to take my daughter to school and I've the baby to feed and everything before I go to work. My husband travels abroad a lot. I have to do everything myself and I work full time.

N: I understand it's not easy for you Dina.

D: I'm sorry. I get a bit emotional sometimes.

N: That's OK. Take your time. Do you want a tissue?

D: Thanks.

N: So, tell me, how is the pain at the moment?

D: OK, I suppose.

N: Good, that's good. This is a Pain Scale. I want you to tell me, from one to ten, how bad is the pain?

D: I'd say two at the moment, but in the morning it's easily seven or eight.

N: That's quite high.

D: It is, yeah.

14

[N = Nurse; D = Dina]

Part 3

N: I want to ask you a few more questions. I hope the baby is OK?

D: She's fine, thanks.
N: OK, so does the pain move at all?
D: Yeah, like I said, I also get this shooting or electric pain that goes down my leg.
N: Right. The doctor will ask you more about that, later. Tell me, what makes the pain worse?
D: Well, I suppose when I lift heavy objects. I have to be careful or it starts up again. The same when I carry my little girl, it starts to hurt again.
N: And what makes it better?
D: If I lie down or take a shower – the heat seems to ease it a little.
N: That's good. Do you have any other problems as a result of the pain?
D: I don't sleep very well and then with the baby, I just get so tired.
N: What about your appetite? How's that?
D: I prepare the kids food, but I don't get time to really eat properly myself. As I said, my husband is away a lot and when he's here I tend to get very angry with him when I'm in pain.

🔊 15

1 Hello Mr Wright. Come in and have a seat.
2 Hello Arthur. Come in and have a seat.
3 Good afternoon, Denny. How can I help you?
4 Good afternoon, Mr Piper. How can I help you?

🔊 16

Hello, Mr Wright. Come in and have a seat.
Good afternoon, Mr Piper. How can I help you?

🔊 17

[A = Angie; C = Carlos]
A: What do you think? I don't like taking painkillers unless they're really necessary.
C: Yes but ginger? I've never heard of using ginger for pain relief. I thought it was for colds and stomach ache.
A: No, you can also use it as an anti-inflammatory. Herb therapy has been around for thousands of years. It's one of the oldest medical treatments ever used. Ginger is great for aching muscles and some of its characteristics are similar to prescription drugs.
C: Really?
A: Sure. Anyway, I think it's better to take herbal therapies than chemicals, don't you?
C: It depends what it is.
A: You suffer from back pain, don't you? What do you take?
C: I tried hypnotherapy once and hydrotherapy.
A: Hy-what?
C: Hydrotherapy – it means therapies using water – swimming, for example. Swimming increases circulation and relaxes the muscles. It's one of the best forms of low-impact exercise, especially for back pain.
A: Swimming is my one of my favourite sports. It sounds like a good idea *and* it's cheap.
C: True. But for me, the best way to relieve back pain is chiropractic therapy.
A: I'm not so sure. What happens exactly?
C: A chiropractor cracks your back to put the bones of your spine back in line. Then gives you advice on exercise and diet.
A: Argh, no thanks. It sounds more painful than the backache.
C: A lot of these therapies are more effective for acute pain than for chronic pain.
A: What about music therapy? That sounds much more relaxing.
C: Are you joking?

Unit 3 Vital signs

🔊 18

[N = Nurse; P = Patient]
1 N: Can you stand here while I measure you please. OK, that's one metre, sixty. Thanks, you can step down now.
2 N: How much do you usually weigh, Martin?
P: Around seventy-two kilos, I think.
3 N: How tall are you now, Laurie?
P: I'm one metre, thirty-four centimetres.
4 P: I've put on a few kilos lately.
N: Well, let's take a look. OK … you're at eighty-nine point five kilos at the moment, Joan.
5 N: Can you put baby Mathew on the scales please, Kelly? Thanks, that's great. Let's see. He now weighs twenty-two point two five kilos. He's doing OK.
6 N: Now let's see how much you've grown since last time … OK – one metre, forty. You've grown over two centimetres!

🔊 19

[N = Nurse; P = Patient]
1 N: Can you empty your bladder first?
P: I went to the toilet a few minutes ago.
N: OK. Can you tell me, how tall are you?
P: Six foot two.
N: And, what's your height in metres?
P: Oh, I'm not sure, sorry. I never remember.
N: Let's check on the scale here. That's one metre eighty-eight. Can you just stand on the scales for me please? OK … yes, that's sixty-five kilos.
P: Sorry, I'm not used to kilos.
N: Sixty-five kilos. That's just over ten stone.
P: Ten stone. Is that all?
N: You sound a little surprised. How much do you weigh normally?
P: Last time I came, I weighed about eleven stone.
2 N: Can you give me your height and weight please?
P: Um, my height – I'm around one metre eighty, I think.
N: OK, that's about average – and how much do you weigh?
P: A hundred and eighty-five pounds - I'm sorry – I'm not used to kilos.
N: I'll look at the chart. Yes, that's eighty kilos.
3 N: So, you're … one point seventy-five metres tall. Let me just note that on your Admission card. OK. And can you just step onto the scales now, please. Yes, and oh … ninety-two kilos. Thank you.
4 N: So, little Jamie is now eighty-six centimetres and let's see how much he weighs. That's twelve point eight kilos. Very good.

🔊 20

1 A digital blood pressure monitor is used to measure a patient's blood pressure.
2 A thermometer is used to measure a patient's body temperature.
3 A pulse oximetre is used to measure how much oxygen there is in a patients's blood – the oxygen saturation.
4 A stethoscope is used by a nurse to listen to heart sounds.
5 A sphygmomanometer is used to measure a patient's blood pressure.

🔊 21

[N = Nurse; CN = Charge Nurse]
1 CN: I can't find Mr Jamieson's Obs Chart.
N: It's in the ward. I'll go and get it.
CN: Thanks. Got it? I want to check his Obs for the last hour.

N: Right, so his temperature is at thirty-seven, so that's OK. Pulse is at 128 and Respiration rate is still high at thirty-three breaths per minute.
CN: And his blood pressure? It was 220 over 140.
N: It's 120 over 80 now.

[N = Nurse; Z = Dr Zhou]
2
N: Hello, is that Mr Zhou?
Z: It is; how can I help you?
N: Your registrar asked me to pass on the latest readings for your patient. She's thinks there's a problem.
Z: Ah, you mean Daniel Samson. Can you read them out to me?
N: Sure. His pulse is seventy-eight beats per minute, temperature thirty-seven point five, blood pressure is eighty-nine over sixty-six and Respiration rate is twenty.
Z: OK? Tell Dr Clement I'll be down in a minute. Thanks.

22

[P = Paediatrician; N = Nurse]
P: How's little Anja today?
N: She's a lot better. Her temp is down to thirty-seven point five.
P: That's good. Can you tell me the rest?
N: Yeah, Resps twenty-five, pulse, stable 130 and BP 100 over 65.
P: Sorry, I didn't quite hear the Pulse. Did you say 120 or 130?
N: 130.

23

[CN = Charge Nurse; D = Debbie]
1
CN: Debbie can you bring us up to date on Rose?
D: Rose Stevens? Sure. Rose suffers from hypertension. So when she came in this morning, her blood pressure was up at 160/100. We monitored her all morning.
CN: And how's she doing now?
D: Much better. Her BP is down from 160/100 to 120/80.
2
CN: Davina Choudhry?
D: Yes, little Davina came in at 2am with her dad. Her temperature was up to thirty-eight point two.
CN: At …?
D: Sorry, yes, her temperature's stable now. It's been at thirty-seven point two since about 10am.
3
D: Can I just tell you about Pilar Chiang?
CN: Go on.
D: Pilar is still wheezing a lot and she's getting very anxious. Her Resps are still up and down. They vary between twenty-five and thirty.
CN: OK, thanks for letting us know, Debbie. Let's keep her on thirty-minute Obs for now.

24

1 Could you just open your mouth for me, please?
2 Can you put your head on one side?
3 Can you just roll up your sleeve for me?
4 Can you give me your right hand please?
5 Could you relax and breathe normally for me?
6 Could you hold your arm out straight?

25

[S = Stefano; P = Patient]
S: I'll take your pulse now, Mr Daniels, if I can? Can you give me your palm, please? I'll put my fingers on your wrist so I can count the beats per minute.
P: It might be higher than usual; I was a bit late for my appointment.
S: You're right, that's ninety-five beats per minute – it is a little high. Can you rest for a few minutes and I'll take a second reading.

26

[S = Stefano; C = Cameron]
S: Ready for your Obs Cameron? Can you give me your right hand please? I'll just clip this little meter to your finger … That's right.
C: Will it hurt?
S: No it won't. It will be very quick, I promise. 110. OK, all done Cameron. I'll just write this down and then we'll take your temperature.

27

[SN = Staff Nurse; A = Ana]
SN: Good morning Ana, how are you feeling today? Sleep OK?
A: Not so bad. I'm a bit hungry though.
SN: The auxiliary is coming round with the breakfast trolley in a few minutes, so I'll do your Obs first, if that's OK?
A: Yes, of course.
SN: Can you sit up for me, please … Good, are you comfortable? I'll take your temperature first. Can you just put this under your tongue please? Let's take your pulse at the same time. Can you give me your right hand please? I'm going to use a little machine called a pulse oximeter.
A: Oh, OK. I've never seen one of those.
N: It will measure your pulse rate. I'll just clip the meter to your finger. That's right. OK, I'll just record that on your chart first and then we'll do your blood pressure. So, that's Resps at seventeen, Pulse eighty and thirty-eight for your temperature.
A: Is that good or bad?
SN: Well, your temperature is still a little high. Dr Baxter will be here later on this morning. She'll give you more information.

28

[SN = Staff Nurse; A = Ana]
SN: OK, to take your blood pressure now?
A: Yeah, sure.
SN: I'll just roll your sleeve up a little. That's good. We'll put a pillow on your lap. Can you hold your arm out straight for me? You can rest it on the pillow. I'll wrap the cuff round your arm. Just relax, that's right. You won't feel any pain; it'll just be a bit tight around your arm. OK? That's 130/85. I'll just take the cuff off now and you can eat your breakfast in peace! I'll see you later.

29

| 1 aorta | 3 vena cava | 5 ventricle |
| 2 artery | 4 atrium | 6 pulmonary |

Unit 4 Symptoms

30

1 Aisha was playing outside this afternoon and she started having difficulty breathing. She was coughing a lot and she said her chest felt tight. She took her blue inhaler, didn't you Aisha. But as it didn't seem to get any better, I brought her in. I've never seen her asthma as bad as this.

2 Yeah, well I was just coming up the main street on my bike when this little kid ran out into the road. I wasn't going very fast but I had to brake hard and I came off my bike. I've got lots of cuts and bruises on my right arm. But it's my eye that's the worst – it's so badly bruised I can't open it. Can I get it checked by the doctor?

3 Yes, I'm a sous chef at Bessie's Place. Do you know it? Great Caribbean food, you must go. Anyway I was working in the kitchens this morning and I cut myself really badly with a chopping knife. It didn't hurt very much at the time but it sure does now. It often bleeds a lot when I cut myself but then it stops usually. I just can't get the bleeding to stop this time. The knife wasn't very clean though and I was worried about infection.

4 I fell off my ladder when I was painting. My shoulder is very swollen and painful and my wrist doesn't look right. I can't move my fingers – that means I've broken something doesn't it? I banged my head really hard when I fell and I still feel dizzy and nauseous.

5 It's my little girl, Jasmine. She had another bad night last night and she's cried nearly all day. I think she's got colic. She seems to have really bad stomach pains – she keeps arching her back and crying. Twice I gave her milk, but she was sick almost immediately both times.

6 I was getting out of the bath when the chest pains started. I felt a sharp stabbing pain in my chest and suddenly it was difficult to breathe. I was very breathless and I also started feeling very dizzy. I almost fell down but I called my wife to come and help me.

🔊 31

[N = Nurse; P = Patient]
N: So Mr Daniels, how would you describe the pain in your chest?
P: Well, it was very difficult to breathe and I felt as if like there was a heavy weight on my chest.
N: Can you explain where exactly?
P: In my chest. Yes, right here in the centre of my chest
N: I see. On a scale of one to ten, how bad was the pain?
P: It wasn't as bad this time – let's say four or five.
N: Four or five? Would you say that was moderate or severe?
P: Moderate, I think.
N: And does the pain move at all?
P: Move? Um … yes, I suppose it does.
N: Go on …
P: It moves down my left arm, sometimes it moves up – I feel it up the left side of my face …
N: OK. How long did the pain last this time?
P: I don't know exactly, around three minutes probably, not that long.
N: Can you tell me how it started?
P: I was carrying something in the shop where I work. I work in a big supermarket. They often ask me to carry heavy things. It's part of the job.
N: I see. Now, how often do you have these pains, Mr Daniels? You said that this isn't the first time?
P: Yes, this is the third time. I've had them for two months now.
N: Do you have any other symptoms? I can hear you're having problems with your breathing.
P: Yes, there's that, but no other problems, no.
N: OK, I've just a couple more questions for you. What seems to make the pain better?
P: If I sit down and rest I usually feel a lot better.
N: Right. Is there anything that makes it worse?
P: If I'm worried or stressed, I've noticed its worse.
N: How do you feel about your condition, Mr Daniels?
P: Well, I'm very worried, nurse. I …

🔊 32

[N = Nurse; A = Ahmed]
1 N: Can you tell me how it happened?
A: I don't know. I was playing really well and then I slipped and fell.
N: How many times has this happened?
A: This is the first time.
N: Does it hurt when I touch here?
A: Arrgh, yes, it's really sore …

N: On a scale of one to ten, how bad is the pain?
A: Five, I guess.

[N = Nurse; V = Vicky]
2 N: Ooo that looks painful. Tell me what happened.
V: I was just doing my kickboxing class at the gym.
N: Do you have any other symptoms?
V: I'm not sure. What do you mean?
N: Dizziness or nausea, for example.
V: I feel a little sick.

🔊 33

[N = Nurse; J = Mr Jenkins; K = Kyle]
N: Hello Kyle, Mr Jenkins. Glad you could come to the clinic today. How are things?
J: Kyle's had a couple of attacks since we saw you last week.
N: Right, so when was the last one, Kyle?
K: Sunday.
N: Sunday, OK, and can you tell me what were you doing when it happened?
K: Playing football with Dad in the park.
N: How long did it last, do you remember?
K: I dunno, about ten minutes.
J: A bit less I think Nurse. Seven minutes, no more.
N: What symptoms do you have when you get these attacks?
K: My chest feels all tight.
N: OK, and how did you try to control the attacks?
K: I used my inhaler … the blue one.
N: The reliever inhaler, that's good. Your best friend is asthmatic too isn't he?
J: His cousin.
N: Ah, my mistake. What I'd just like to do now if that's OK is to check how Kyle is using his inhaler. I want to make sure he knows how to use it properly.
J: That sounds like a good idea, doesn't it Kyle. Just to be on the safe side.

🔊 34

First, sit down at a table. Don't lie down. Then, lead forward slightly and put your arms on the table. Next, take up to six puffs of your inhaler. Call an ambulance after six minutes if your symptoms don't improve. Then, continue to take your inhaler every six minutes, for a maximum of six puffs. Finally, repeat these steps, if your symptoms begin again.

Unit 5 Food and nutrition

🔊 35

[N = Nurse; A = Alain]
N: What's your normal weight, Alain?
A: I'm about seventy-five kilos, I guess.
N: I see my colleague weighed you earlier and you're currently around sixty-six kilos. OK, and how tall are you?
A: About one metre seventy-two.
N: Mmm, that gives you a BMI of around twenty-two point four. What weight would you like to be?
A: The same as before, seventy-five.
N: I just need to ask you a few questions, if I may. Erm, do you have any food allergies we should know about?
A: Yes, I'm allergic to peanuts.
N: That's important for us to know, thanks. Anything else? What about lactose intolerance?
A: I'm sorry?
N: Dairy products. Do you have any problems digesting dairy products, like milk?
A: No, no I can drink milk. I don't like cheese though.
N: OK. When was your last meal?
A: About ten, last night, when I finished work. A bowl of soup, some toast …

[N = Nurse; A = Alain]

N: Your calorie intake is very low in general and because of this you're not getting the energy you need to do your job. It's not a balanced diet; you lack protein, carbohydrates and fibre. Unhealthy eating patterns are a common problem for busy people.

A: I get very tired and sometimes I have problems remembering things, which is serious in my job.

N: Very true. Also, you're skipping breakfast, which means you're missing the most important meal of the day. After eight to ten hours without food, your body needs energy. And you're drinking quite a lot of coffee.

A: I know; I need it to wake me up.

N: But there are some positive things about your diet. Brown bread is a good source of fibre and you do eat three portions of fruit and vegetables a day, which is not bad. You don't eat a lot of snacks, and the only snack you took yesterday was a piece of fruit.

🔘 37

[N = Nurse; A = Alain]

N: Let's look at the kind of foods you could bring to work. Fresh fruit and vegetables of course. Yoghurts are very practical and high in protein. And avocados are a good choice too. They're high in calories, high in fibre, potassium and fat.

A: I love food normally, but working as a nurse on the night shift, it's really difficult to eat a balanced meal.

🔘 38

1 My son has lots of food allergies.
2 She has a severe allergic reaction to nuts.
3 I had a pain in my abdomen.
4 Do you suffer from abdominal pain?
5 His respiratory system was affected.
6 Respiration is one of the vital signs.

🔘 39

[N = Nurse; J = Joely]

N: First, it's important to ask your patient's permission to check their blood sugar. We always need to do this before a procedure.

J: OK

N: After that, the next thing to do is to put a testing strip into the glucometer. When the glucometer is ready, ask the patient to hold out a finger.

J: Is it important which finger?

N: No, any finger is OK. Make sure the patient knows what is happening and tell them that you are going to prick their finger with your lancet. Prick the top of the finger and get a drop of blood which you put on the test strip. Then, put the test strip into the glucometer – don't forget to give your patient a cotton swab for their finger. Wait for a few moments for the glucometer to work. Then you'll see the results of the test come up on the screen.

🔘 40

The government advises us to eat five portions of fruit and veg a day, but what do they mean by a portion? One portion of fresh fruit can be one apple, fourteen cherries or two slices of mango. If you eat canned fruit at home, then eight segments of grapefruit is considered a portion, for example. And for dried fruit – try one tablespoon of raisins or two figs. A medium glass of fruit juice or a small carton – that's 150 ml – counts as one portion.

Portions of vegetables are a little more difficult to count. If you like salads – then three sticks of celery counts as one portion. Three tablespoons of cooked, canned or frozen vegetables is also one portion.

So far so good. Now for the bad news. I'm sure there are a lot of you who like chips or a packet of crisps in front of your favourite film – me too. Sorry to say that potato and other starchy vegetables, like yams, cannot be included in the five a day.

Finally, be careful of ready-meals and takeaways. They may contain vegetables but they are also high in salt and sugar. And even if you think they include lots of different vegetables, they only count as one portion!

Now, let's see if I can answer your questions …

🔘 41

[N = Nurse; L = Lena]

1 N: Good to see you Lena. How have you been this week?

L: I still don't have much energy, but I want to get back to work as soon as I can. I wanted to ask you about a diet plan. I've never lost weight before. I was 57 kilos and now I'm only 50.

N: Well this is common with glandular fever but you do need to build up your appetite again. Can I suggest you eat little and often at first. And it's important to drink lots of water.

[N = Nurse; F = Frank]

2 F: Thank you for agreeing to see me today.

N: That's OK. Dr Sanchez said you wanted to talk about improving your diet.

F: She said something about a Mediterranean diet, is that right?

N: Yes. A Mediterranean diet will help reduce your risk of another heart attack.

F: I'm not sure I'm going to like it though. I don't like many vegetables. I'm a real meat eater.

N: You can eat some red meat, just not too much. Why don't you try eating fish – sardines, salmon – instead of meat? Could you try those instead?

F: I guess so.

N: It won't be easy at first – it takes time …

[N = Nurse; E = Edith]

3 N: How long have you been on the weight loss programme Edith?

E: About two months now, but it's not working. I can't lose the weight.

N: Are you doing any exercise, Edith, can I ask?

E: I've never really liked sport. Jogging, the gym – it's not for me.

N: It is important to exercise if you want to lose weight, Edith. How about walking the dog?

E: My son does that normally.

N: Can I suggest you go with your son. Adults should do 30 minutes of exercise five times a week.

Unit 6 Personal care

🔘 42

[N = Nurse; T = Mrs Turner]

1 N: Mrs Turner, I can see you're a bit breathless today, so I'm going to help you get ready this morning.

T: Oh are you dear? Thanks ever so much. My son is bringing my grandchildren round this afternoon. I want to wash and be ready for them.

N: Is he, that's lovely – something to look forward to. I'm just going to pull the curtain round your bed and give you some privacy. That's better. Do you need help brushing your teeth?

T: I think I can do that by myself.

N: OK, good. Here's a swab to clean your teeth. I'm going to put this kidney basin on the table in front of you. You can spit into it when you're finished. OK let's have a little rest now.

M: Oh, good idea. I'm tired this morning.

[N = Nurse; M = Mary]

2 N: Good morning, Mary. Sleep OK?

M: Not so well, nurse. I just don't have any energy at all today.

N: I'm sorry to hear that. Let's see if we can make you feel a little better. Are you ready for your wash?

M: If you like.

N: Well, here's a washcloth for your face and I'm going to find a towel for you. Is the water OK for you? Not too hot?

M: Fine thanks.

N: You're doing well Mary. Here's your towel. Great, now lie back and rest before we brush your hair. OK here's the brush and I'm going to place the mirror on the table for you. Can you see OK?

M: Yes, thanks.

🎧 **43**

[N = Nurse; K = Mr Karam]

1 N: Good morning Mr Karam. How did you sleep?

K: Not so bad, thanks.

N: Do you need any help with getting washed and dressed this morning?

K: I think I'm OK with the shower; I can wash by myself, but I just need some help with shaving, please. My hands are shaky and it's difficult to hold the razor still without cutting myself.

N: Not to worry. Ring the buzzer when you're ready and I'll give you a hand. Do you have a clean razor?

K: Yes, there's some in my locker that my son brought in for me.

[N = Nurse; E = Eileen]

2 E: Excuse me nurse, could you give me a hand?

N: Of course. What do you need help with, Elaine?

E: I'm having problems with dressing. My back hurts when I bend down, but I can't put my tights on without bending down.

N: That's OK, I can help you with that. There you go, that's done. Do you need help with anything else?

E: I had a bath, but I didn't wash my hair. Could you give me a hand with washing my hair, it's difficult to reach?

N: Yes Elaine, just give me a minute, I'll go and get a washbowl and jug.

E: I don't have any shampoo left.

N: Conditioner?

E: Please …

[N = Nurse; S = Samson]

3 N: Samson, Hi. Are you OK or do you need help with getting ready this morning?

S: I'm OK, thanks.

N: Are you sure? Do you need help cleaning your teeth?

S: It's OK, I can do it.

N: Getting dressed?

S: No, thanks. I want to try and do everything by myself today.

N: That's good news. I'm going to sit at the nurse's desk. If you need anything, just ring the buzzer.

S: Sorry, Nurse Sheldon?

N: Yes?

S: I can't find my toothbrush …

[N = Nurse; B = Mr Bates]

4 B: Nurse, nurse, I'm sorry can you help me; I need help with getting to the toilet.

N: Just a second, Mr Bates. I'm going to bring the commode to you.

B: No, no, I prefer to go to the toilet. Is that OK? I really don't like using that thing.

N: I can understand.

B: I'm just so pleased, I don't have to use the bed pan anymore. That was terrible!

N: Umm. Do you think you can walk over by yourself or do you need the walker?

B: It's better if I take the walker, I think.

N: Now take your time, Mr Bates, that's it. Slowly does it. I'm just going to close the door, give you a bit of privacy.

🎧 **44**

[N = Nurse; S = Shaminder]

1 N: Shaminder, how are you doing?

S: I can't hold the knife and fork properly, nurse. I've been trying to eat this omelette for ten minutes now. It's so frustrating.

N: I understand how you must be feeling. Do you want me to come back later?

S: No, no. I'm not sure.

N: How about I give you a spoon instead? You can take your time.

S: Yes, but everyone can see. It's a bit humiliating.

N: I'll bring a screen to put round the bed. You can have a little privacy. What do you think?

S: OK.

N: Let me know if you need any help.

[N = Nurse; S = Sheila]

2 P: I'm so sorry nurse. My hands were shaking and …

N: I can see exactly what's happened Sheila – you've dropped the jug and now there's water all over the floor. Why didn't you call me?

S: I … I don't know. I … I thought you were busy.

N: We're always busy, aren't we dear? Now I have to clean this mess up as well.

S: Sorry nurse, I'm a bit embarrassed.

N: Don't be embarrassed, Sheila. It can happen to anyone. Next time, just please ring the buzzer when you need help washing your hair … OK?

[J = Josh; N = Nurse]

3 J: Oh, how embarrassing. I am so sorry. Please excuse me, I didn't mean to. I know it's the chemo that's making me sick, but it's actually quite depressing.

N: Please don't worry, Josh. The sickness won't last. Let me clean you up and you'll feel much better.

J: OK, thank you. You're so understanding.

N: I can see it's difficult for you, but I'm used to it; it's part of my job. Now, I'm just going to give you some water to rinse your mouth. Is that better?

J: Yes, thanks.

N: Do you need a clean T-shirt? No, you're OK, good. Do you want to watch some TV?

🎧 **45**

[N = Nurse; P = Patient]

N: Hello. Can you just confirm your name for me?

P: Una Hagans.

N: Great, thanks Ms Hagans. So how are things after your operation? Let's see … you've had your appendix removed – is that right?

P: Yes, the painkillers make me feel a bit nauseous, but I'm OK. Just the area around the wound is a little itchy.

N: Yes it will be; it's a good sign – it means the wound is healing, so there's no infection and you don't need any antibiotics.

P: That's good to know.
N: Sorry, just give me a minute to put on my disposable gloves. Right. Let me see, you've got sutures and we need to change your dressing every day. Before I start, can I just ask you is the wound painful at all?
P: Like I said, it's a bit itchy, but it really doesn't hurt very much. I can hardly feel it at all.
N: So, on a scale of one to ten, how painful is it?
P: Two maybe.
N: Two, OK. Now, I'm just going to remove the old dressing and then we can clean the wound. I'll just pop that in the bin. Ermm, it all looks very clean and healthy … good. There's no pus or bad odour and the edges are joining up nicely.
P: Uh huh.
N: I'm going to use some saline solution just to clean the wound. I'll try to do it gently. Let me know if you want me to stop. OK, Ms Hagans, I'm just going to clean that up and put the absorbent dressing on. How's that for you?
P: Good, yes, thanks.
N: I just need to secure the dressing with some tape. There we go. Let me just fill in your wound assessment chart and we're done.

Unit 7 Elimination

🎵 46

[N = Nurse; T = Toni]
1 N: How have you been for the last few days, Toni?
  T: Well, it's a bit embarrassing really.
  N: Go on …
  T: Well, I've had problems with my waterworks again.
  N: I see. And have you passed water today?
  T: Yes, but only a few drops. I never manage to empty my bladder.

[N = Nurse; L = Leah, A = Mrs Azra]
2 N: Leah, did you do a pooh this morning?
  A: Tell the nurse, honey …
  L: No.
  N: No? And did you go to the toilet yesterday?
  L: Yes.
  N: Was that for a pooh or a wee?
  T: I did a wee wee.
  N: Did you? Well done. When was the last time she passed a stool?
  L: About a week ago, I think.
  N: Mrs Azra, have you noticed any blood in Leah's motions?
  A: A little, yeah.
  N: Has she been in any pain?
  A: Yes, yes she has. It's a bit worrying.
  N: Can you describe the stool?
  A: Well, its kind of …

[N = Nurse; D = Dave]
3 D: Yes, nurse, I've come to get something for my stomach?
  N: What seems to be the problem?
  D: Well, basically, I've had the runs ever since I came back from holiday. Maybe I ate something bad or I've caught some kind of infection, I'm not sure.
  N: I see. How long have you had the diarrhoea exactly?
  D: Since Tuesday evening.
  N: OK And did you eat anything when you were on holiday that you think could have given you diarrhoea?
  D: I ate quite a lot of shellfish …
  N: That sounds like a possibility. Now, how many times have you had a bowel movement today, Dave?
  D: About four or five times.
  N: Can you describe the stool?
  D: I'm sorry …?

🎵 47

[N = Nurse; S = Ms Sonoda]
N: Is there anything else Ms Sonoda; you look a bit worried?
S: Erm, I'm sorry; it's very embarrassing for me to talk about.
N: Don't worry, take your time.
S: I have some pain.
N: Pain?
S: Yes, I have pains, just here when I go to the toilet and then it stops.
N: Could you explain what you mean?
S: Well, I go to the toilet and it's very painful. But then afterwards the pain is gone.
N: I see. And can you describe your bowel movements?
S: Erm, yes. No, I'm sorry …
N: I understand this isn't an easy thing to talk about. A normal bowel movement is where there is no pain and the stools are soft and easy to pass.
S: No, no, its not like that.
N: OK. When you go to the toilet are the stools small and hard or runny?
S: Well, very runny.

🎵 48

[N = Nurse; C = Christophe]
Part 1
N: Morning Christophe. How are you feeling?
C: Not great.
N: Really?
C: Sorry, it's a bit embarrassing.
N: Take your time.
C: I feel bloated.
N: How long have you felt like this?
C: A couple of days.
N: Have you opened your bowels today?
C: No, not today.
N: So, when did you last open your bowels?
C: I haven't been to the toilet since the operation.
N: And how often do you usually go?
C: Every day. I'm pretty regular.
N: How long have been in hospital now?
C: They operated on me a week ago. I've been here since the 5th May.
N: Well, you've not been very active since the operation, that's probably the reason. But it's quite normal, Christophe, a lot of people suffer from constipation after an operation. It'll take just a bit of time to get back to your normal bowel pattern.

🎵 49

[N = Nurse; C = Christophe]
Part 2
N: Have you eaten anything?
C: No, I didn't eat anything last night. I didn't have much of an appetite.
N: What about breakfast this morning?
C: I drank the orange juice, but that's all.
N: OK. And what was your stool like on Sunday?
C: Um, small, hard lumps. I pushed a lot, too.
N: What is it like usually?
C: I don't know … normal, soft, I guess.
N: Did you feel any pain?
C: No, no pain.
N: Any pain in your abdomen?
C: None at all, no.
N: Ah, well that's good. Listen, I'll ask the doctor to prescribe you some laxatives. Try to drink more water and we can talk about diet later.

I work for a medical charity and at the moment I'm working in a refugee camp in North East Africa. It's not an easy place to be. The camp was made to for about 1,000 people, but there is more than than twice that number. We don't have enough clean water and there are problems with outbreaks of sickness and diarrohea. As you know infection is spread through dirty drinking water and that was one of the biggest problems here at the beginning. The most important thing in treating diarrhoea is to rehydate the patient. A severely dehydrated patient needs rehydration with intravenous fluids. They go into the hospital here and have an intravenous drip. For moderate dehydration, it is possible to treat a patient effectively with oral rehydration salts or ORS. We have saved a lot of lives, particularly children's lives with this. ORS is a mixture of clean water, salt and sugar which is very easy to prepare even here where we have such limited medical facilities. It's very cheap, which is also important. As I often have to explain, ORS does not stop the diarrhoea but it stops the dangerous dehydration caused by the diarrhoea. It is absorbed in the small intestine and replaces the water and electrolytes lost in the faeces.

51

[N = Nurse; A = Anita]
Part 1
N: Anita Blasky? Hello, can you come with me? Would you like to sit down? Can I call you Anita?
A: If you like.
N: Anita, can you tell me what has brought you here today?
A: Um, well, you know, it's kind of embarrassing really.
N: Don't worry, take your time.
A: I … I don't feel very well.
N: Could you explain what you mean?
A: I've had stomach ache for a few days and problems going to the toilet.
N: What kind of problems?
A: It's like, I want to go all the time. And sometimes …
N: Sometimes?
A: Sometimes, I … I just like don't get there in time, you know … to the toilet.
N: I see. I understand it must be difficult for you.
A: Yeah. It's just so embarrassing.
N: OK, we'll come back to this in a second. I'm just going to ask you a few questions about your bowel movements first, if that's OK.

52

[N = Nurse; A = Anita]
Part 2
N: What about food, have you eaten anything spicy in the last couple of days?
A: No, no I haven't. I don't really like spicy foods; I only eat it at family parties.
N: And do you have any food allergies?
A: I don't know what you mean?
N: Well, some people suffer from diarrhoea if they eat or drink milk products for example?
A: No, no I don't really drink milk.
N: Have you noticed a change in your weight recently?
A: Why are you asking about my weight all of a sudden?
N: It's just one of the questions I have to ask. How do you feel about your weight, Anita?
A: I … I'm overweight – I mean for my height, you know. And anyway, I need to lose some more.
N: And how much weight have you lost?
A: About five kilos. This girl at college, she told me about using … laxatives.
N: Laxatives?

Unit 8 Patient discharge

53

Jim broke his leg in a skiing accident. He doesn't really remember what happened. It was a bad fall and he broke his leg in two places. It's still in plaster so it's not easy for him to walk. He's using crutches to help get around.

Mrs Ridley has had a hip operation. It was successful, but she needs time to get better and recover her strength. She's 78 and rather frail. She can't walk very far, so she uses a wheelchair when she goes out. Her husband is strong enough to push her.

Elin is an artist. She fell off a ladder when she was working on a big wall painting and hurt her back. She was completely paralysed for awhile. She's had a lot of physiotherapy and has recovered her mobility more than we thought was possible. She needs to wear a leg brace because her right leg was badly damaged and she uses a walking stick to help her get around.

Mr Aziz has arthritis in his legs. He's been in hospital for some drug treatment, to which he responded well. His knees are still quite painful, however, and he can't get around very quickly. He uses a walking frame to give him some support when he's out by himself.

54

[N = Nurse; R = Mr Ridley]
1 N: Your wife is very frail, Mr Ridley and she's going to need help with going to the toilet, for example.
   R: Yes, I realize that. But it's going to be difficult for me to lift her on and off the toilet.
   N: Yes. If you get a raised toilet seat, she'll be able to slide from her wheelchair onto the toilet. That'll make it easier for you too.
   R: Erm, I'll look into it.

[N = Nurse; A = Arto]
2 N: Your sister will need help getting in and out of the bath.
   A: Yes, I'm a bit worried about that. She'll fall if she's not careful; I know what she's like.
   N: She could quite easily, yes. It's a good idea to install grab bars around the bath, so she can hold on to them as she gets in and out of the bath. And if she has a non-slip mat, it'll stop her from slipping. Does she have one?
   A: No.
   N: I strongly advise you to get one. They're not expensive.
   A: You're right. If we have time, we'll visit the local DIY store on the way home.

[N = Nurse; J = Jim]
3 N: So, you're leaving tomorrow, Jim. Good news!
   J: I know. It's too cool!
   N: So how do you feel about washing and dressing? Do you feel strong enough to do this by yourself today? You need to practice before we discharge you.
   J: Yeah, sure, why not, I'll give it a go. But if I stand for a long time, I get tired.
   N: Well, there's a shower chair in the bathroom. Why don't you try taking your shower sitting down today? If you need help, just press the buzzer.

55

[N = Nurse; N = Nancy]
N: So, Nancy, we're going to look at your Discharge Plan together. I'm going to explain what's going to happen and if you have any questions, just ask. OK?

N: I'm a bit worried about going home, Nurse. I live alone and I'm not sure if I'll manage by myself.

N: Do you have a friend or family member who could help you, perhaps?

N: I know my sister will help me if I have problems and maybe my neighbour, if necessary.

N: That's good. How do you feel about getting to the toilet and getting dressed by yourself?

N: I think I'll be OK, I've been managing by myself with the toilet and I can get dressed if things are easy to reach.

N: Could your sister perhaps prepare your clothes for you every evening?

N: Yes, I suppose she could. What about washing? I'm worried I'll fall if I'm not careful.

N: Be sure to put a non-slip mat in the shower and maybe a couple of grab bars as well.

N: Grab bars? What are they?

N: You put them around the shower and you can hold on to them to stop yourself from slipping.

N: Oh, OK, I know. That's a good idea.

N: How about preparing meals? Are you worried about that at all?

N: Yes, that's the thing I'm most worried about. If I feel as tired as I am today, I won't have the energy for cooking.

N: That's true. If you start feeling tired, make sure you rest – that's very important. Try to eat at least one piece of fruit every day and drink lots of water. But perhaps your sister could prepare some meals in advance? You can heat them up when you want.

N: Uh huh.

N: Now, you can't drive again for another three to four weeks. If you need help with the shopping will your neighbour do it, perhaps?

N: Yes, I'm sure he would.

🎧 56

[N = Nurse; N = Nancy]

N: How do you feel about going home today, Nancy?

N: I was a bit worried yesterday, but I feel better today. It was good to look at the Discharge Plan together.

N: Good! Now, I just want to talk to you now about your medications, if that's OK. I'm going to give you a list. Your doctor will give you some capsules and some tablets. The capsules are antibiotics. These are very important because they will stop you getting an infection. You need to take two capsules, three times a day at mealtimes.

N: OK.

N: The tablets are painkillers. If you're in pain, then take two tablets. But don't take more than two every six hours, and no more than eight tablets a day. There's also a tube of antiseptic ointment. You need to put this on twice a day – in the morning when you get up and at night when you go to bed. Apply it to the area where your stitches are.

N: Right, is all this written down?

N: Yes. Don't worry it's all on the list. Oh, and I forgot. It isn't unusual for patients to suffer from constipation after surgery so the doctor has also prescribed a laxative syrup for you.

N: Oh, good, thank you.

N: You need to take a tablespoonful three times a day at mealtimes. Can your sister get your medications from the pharmacy for you?

N: Yes, we can do that on the way home. What's going to happen about my stitches?

N: A home care nurse will be coming to visit you at home the day after tomorrow. She'll change your dressings and make sure you're healing well. Then in ten days you have an appointment in the outpatient clinic. We'll take your stitches out for you then. It's all written down here.

🎧 57

[R = Receptionist; Z = Zafar]

R: Hello, this is the Mount Health Centre, can I help you?

Z: Good afternoon. This is Zafar from Orthopaedics. I'd like to make an appointment with the Practice Nurse for one of our patients, please.

R: Yes, OK. Which day?

Z: I want to book him in for a check-up in about ten days' time please. How about the 23rd?

R: Just a moment, please. I'm sorry, the 23rd is completely booked. Would the 24th January be OK? I have slots at 16.05 and 17.30.

Z: Tuesday the 24th, yes that's fine. Do you have any appointments in the morning?

R: Let me just check. Err, yes, I have a cancellation at 10.15.

Z: Good, so that's 10.15 on the 24th of January. Let me give you the patient's details. It's Mr Ernesto Chavaz, that's C-H-A-V-A-Z.

R: Er-nes-to Cha-vaz. OK, got that. Thanks.

Z: Thank you for your help. Goodbye.

🎧 58

[R = Receptionist; Z = Zafar]

R: Occupational Therapy, good afternoon.

Z: Good afternoon. This is Zafar from Orthopaedics.

R: Hi Zafar, how are you? It's Sandra.

Z: Ah, Sandra, good. I'm fine, thanks. Listen, I'd like to make an appointment for Geoff Pattern to see an occupational therapist.

R: Sure, when can he make the first appointment? Our therapist is only here on Tuesdays and Thursdays.

Z: Right. Erm, how about next Tuesday, sometime in the afternoon?

R: We can fit him in any time after three thirty.

Z: OK, what about five o'clock?

R: No problem. Tuesday, 17th June at five o'clock. Can you give me the patient's details, please?

Z: Of course. Geoff, G-E-O-double F, Pattern, P-A-double T-E-R-N.

🎧 59

[R = Receptionist; Z = Zafar]

R: Occupational therapy, Sandra speaking.

Z: Hi Sandra, it's Zafar again. Sorry to disturb you but can I reschedule Mr Pattern's first appointment? There's a problem and he can't come at the time we arranged.

R: OK, let's see. What time was his appointment?

Z: Tuesday afternoon at 5 pm.

R: Sorry did you say Tuesday or Thursday?

Z: Tuesday, Tuesday afternoon.

R: OK, can you just hang on a moment. I'll check. It'll have to be the morning, I'm afraid. How about Thursday at 10.50?

Z: Thursday at 10.15, that's sounds OK.

R: No, not 10.15, 10.50.

Z: Oh, OK, 10.50, sorry. Yes, that's fine. Thanks a lot.

Pearson Education Limited
Edinburgh Gate
Harlow
Essex CM20 2JE
England

and Associated Companies throughout the world.

www.pearsonelt.com

© Pearson Education Limited 2011

The right of Ros Wright and Maria Spada Symonds to be identified as authors of this Work has been asserted by them in accordance with the Copyright, Designs and Patents Act 1988.

First published 2011

impression 8

ISBN: 978-1-4082-6994-7

Set ITC Cheltenham Book

Printed and bound by Ashford Colour Press Ltd, Gosport, Hampshire.

Acknowledgements

The publishers would like to thank the following people for their helpful comments on the manuscript for this book:

Jean-Pierre Charpy, France; Peggy Labat, France; Shobha Nandagopal, Oman; Samad Sajjadi, Iran

The publisher would like to thank the following for their kind permission to reproduce their photographs:

(Key: b-bottom; c-centre; l-left; r-right; t-top)

p5 Getty Images: 3660 Group Inc. (t). **Photolibrary.com:** Granger Wootz / Blend Images (b). **p11 Alamy Images:** Peter Scholey. **p16 Alamy Images:** Nic Cleave. **p21 Fotolia.com:** Roman A. Kozlov (b); maotun (e). **Pearson Education Ltd:** Photodisc (d). **Science Photo Library Ltd:** Photostock (a); Jim Varney (c). **p23 iStockphoto:** (l). **Thinkstock:** Creatas Images (c); Bananastock (r). **p25 Getty Images:** Sean Justice. **p27 Thinkstock:** iStockphoto. **p30 Alamy Images:** Science Photo Library. **p33 Alamy Images:** ImageState. **p35 Photolibrary.com:** Ismael Lopez / Real Latino Images (r). **SuperStock:** Kablonk (l). **p36 iStockphoto. p37 Alamy Images:** Asia Images Group Pte Ltd (b). **Getty Images:** arabianEye (c). **Photolibrary.com:** Radius Images (a). **Thinkstock:** Bananastock (d). **p38 Alamy Images:** Glowimages. **p40 Thinkstock:** Hemera. **p46 Fotolia.com:** Glenda Powers (3); Marek (5). **Thinkstock:** Jupiter Images (1); iStockphoto (2); Stockbyte (4); Brand X Pictures (6). **p48 Thinkstock:** Jupiter Images. **p51 Science Photo Library Ltd:** Dr. P. Marazzi. **p52 Thinkstock:** Stockbyte. **p53 Pearson Education Ltd:** Lord And Leverett (l); MindStudio (r). **Thinkstock:** iStockphoto. **p54 Photolibrary.com:** ERproductions Ltd. **p55 Getty Images:** Tessa Codrington. **p57 Getty Images:** AFP. **p58 Photofusion Picture Library:** Crispin Hughes (t); Colin Edwards (b). **p60 DK Images:** Stephen Oliver (d). **Patterson Medical Ltd:** (e). **Photofusion Picture Library:** Libby Welch (b); Liam Bailey (c). **Thinkstock:** iStockphoto (a). **p63 Alamy Images:** Bubbles Photolibrary. **p66 Science Photo Library Ltd:** Mark Thomas.

Cover images: *Front:* **Photolibrary.com:** Comstock c, Corbis l, David Trainor Background, Photodisc r

All other images © Pearson Education

Every effort has been made to trace the copyright holders and we apologise in advance for any unintentional omissions. We would be pleased to insert the appropriate acknowledgement in any subsequent edition of this publication.

Picture Research by Kevin Brown